FREEDOM FIGHTERS
— AND —
HELL RAISERS

FREEDOM FIGHTERS

FIGHTERS

AND

HELL

RAISERS

A Gallery of
Memorable Southerners

HAL CROWTHER

BLAIR

Printed in the United States of America
Cover design by Laura Williams
Interior design by April Leidig
Illustrations by Nathan Golub
Blair is an imprint of Carolina Wren Press.

*The mission of Carolina Wren Press is to seek out, nurture,
and promote literary work by new and underrepresented writers.*

We gratefully acknowledge the ongoing support of general operations
by the Durham Arts Council's United Arts Fund.

Library of Congress Cataloging-in-Publication Data
Names: Crowther, Hal, author.
Title: Freedom fighters and hell raisers :
a gallery of memorable southerners / by Hal Crowther.
Description: Durham, NC : Blair/Carolina Wren Press, [2018]
Identifiers: LCCN 2018026070| ISBN 9780932112774 (hc) |
ISBN 9780932112781 | ISBN 9780932112996 (ebook)
Subjects: LCSH: Southern States--Biography. | Southern States--
Civilization. | Southern States--Intellectual life. | LCGFT: Essays.
Classification: LCC F208 .C75 2018 | DDC 975--dc23
LC record available at https://lccn.loc.gov/2018026070

Contents

Foreword

BY SILAS HOUSE

MOST ANYONE HOLDING this book would agree that it is being published in dark days. No matter what you think about the current political climate, I would find it hard to deny the fact that we're witnessing the death rattle of things like nuance, decorum, and honesty. Arrogance—one of the deadly sins when I was growing up—is now celebrated and rewarded with fashion lines, reality shows, and all the likes and retweets that social media can handle. Teachers are being negated by governors and senators. Being smart is now openly made fun of by our so-called leaders as was only done in the past by drooling schoolyard dullards and bullies. Freedom of the press is under daily attack.

"In a dark time," Roethke wrote, "the eye begins to see."

In these troubling times we've seen that the great poet was correct. High schoolers have rallied the entire nation to rethink automatic weapons. Worldwide protests have brought people out into the streets who never before even thought of themselves as anything remotely approaching an activist. Women have changed the world with the recent Time's Up and #MeToo movements. Investigative journalists are doing some of their best work in decades, exposing shocking secrets of politicians and harassers. Thousands of think pieces have been written about our current dilemma. Perhaps best of all, artists are reacting to this gathering storm with films, novels, essays, paintings, music, and other art forms that are forcing people to think complexly, challenging them to offer resuscitation to nuance, to read between the lines, to use their brains.

Hal Crowther has always done that. The essays in this collection were written before our current political crisis, and Crowther was always ahead of the curve when it came to the national conversation. In one of these essays he wrote: "A smug sub-literacy is spreading like dense fog across America's cerebral landscape; when and how it might clear, no one I know is prepared to say." He was warning us of this thickening mist before most others could predict its conjuring. Now that anti-intellectualism is a choking smog in America, his writing is more important than ever. One need only look at the first essay in this collection, written about celebrated writer Molly Ivins, to see how prophetic Crowther's writing has always been. This is something that readers will find happening again and again in collected essays that are perhaps even more relevant now than when they were first written.

Shortly after I read Crowther's book *Cathedrals of Kudzu* in the year 2000, I spent a week with him at a writers' conference, and by the end of that time together I knew I had been in the presence of one of the most intelligent people I had ever met. That's always the way I describe him to everyone. Reading these essays reminds me of what an apt description that is. It is also appropriate that in a time when so many of us are mourning the loss of complex discussion and decorum, among other things, Crowther is giving us a book of essays that have their impetus in death.

He is quick to point out that these are neither obituaries nor eulogies, but essays that "aspire to the virtues of both." I would argue that they go far beyond that. They are profound meditations on the big issues: race (appropriate for a collection by a man I consider as one of the major public intellectuals of the New South, a culture simultaneously embracing progress while also keeping a close eye—and hand—on the past), religion (an essay about a nun, appropriately titled "Confession," becomes a deeply personal look at faith, doubt, and forgiveness), art (a meditation on the death of a preacher is also a rumination on great writing), politics (providing some of his most deliciously biting commentary), social justice, and much more. In a time of "alternative facts," Crowther is focusing on the truth in every single one of these essays. Sometimes his truth is brutal. Always his truth is intelligent, meticulously researched, necessary, and written in his unmistakable voice that manages to be full of authority without ever sounding like a know-it-all. Crowther's voice is sometimes cynical—but only when it needs to be. More often it is full of admiration, logic, and even hope. Always his writing is funny. Jesse Helms, in Crowther's words, is "a huge old pit bull, useless and vicious, that sits in its own mess at the end of a tow-truck chain and snarls at everything that moves." A scene after a college football game is described this way: "boys with thick necks and buzz cuts, liberated from training, stalked the campus in various stages of alcohol poisoning." A study of forgiveness includes this finding: "perhaps testosterone and patience are incompatible."

In all of this writing Crowther is getting at that one most threatened thing in our America today: complexity. These certainly are neither eulogies nor obituaries because those two forms of writing rarely capture as much nuance as Crowther has wrangled so beautifully here. For example, his admiration for the poet James Dickey is clear in "The Last Wolverine," but he is no wearer of rose-colored glasses. He finds the frustrating aspects of the man's existence as important and interesting and as worthy of being told as he does his admirable qualities. We learn not only about Dickey clamping Crowther "in a headlock I couldn't break," but also the writer's inappropriate entitlement on his own sexual indulgences and the dangerous belief that being a genius is a kind of exemption. Anyone who desires a master class in writing about the complexity of a human being—especially one who has come to be a symbol for something as evil as racism—need only look to Crowther's exquisite study of George Wallace where he writes:

> The bantamweight from Clio has thrown his last punch. Under normal circumstances this would be an occasion for stock-taking, a time when the South might find some satisfaction in a moral inventory. The most vivid symbol of its ancestral transgressions is gone—and he departed repentant, shriven and forgiven and ready for whatever grace the next place allows.

This kind of beauty is woven throughout the collection. There's the passage where Crowther tells us about his loyalties to a wonderful poem by James Still being tested by the presence of an emerald hummingbird: "The poem and the bird struggled for my attention, until I imagined a voice I knew as well as the ageless face that I often studied on the sly. 'Set that poem aside,' it said, 'and mind the hummingbird.'" Crowther certainly knows how to turn a phrase, as he did here: "The truly embarrassing people, Martin Luther King, Jr., for instance—or Jesus Christ—can be a greater

force dead than alive. Anne Braden . . . was one of the most embarrassing Southern women who ever lived," perfectly articulating
what it means to be an activist who puts not only her reputation
but also her life on the line for the cause she believes in. In this essay we learn not only about Braden's tireless fight against racism,
but also Crowther's upbringing on the issue. In fact, we are always
firmly rooted in Crowther's point of view on the world, and often
he gives us personal reflections not only from his personal relationships with many of his subjects but also looks into his own life.
Yet there is never anything remotely approaching the navel-gazing
that happens so often in first-person nonfiction writing these days.
Crowther is much too interested in the world and the people in it
for that, and he is a master at making us interested, too.

This is a book we need right now. Not only because it is beautifully written, entrancing, and funny, but perhaps even more so
because it is a book of complexity and truth. Very often it is about
people who are fighting the good fight, whether that be through activism, prayer, or—most often—the arts. When it's not, it's about
the people who needed to be fought against. Crowther, like the best
writers, knows these are times that need more truth, more nuance,
more empathy. In this dark time, he is once again drawing our eyes
to the important matters at hand and articulating them all with
firm grace and keen intelligence—two things we need much more
of right now, and always.

Introduction

THE GRAVESIDE SERVICE, in a grim prairie churchyard or some cinematic cemetery with old trees and broad green lawns, provides dramatic ballast for hundreds of motion pictures. Filmmakers like to shoot the scene from a bird's-eye camera, or zoom in from a great distance on the grief-hushed gathering until we can hear the clergyman's traditional words of cold comfort. It's a foolproof setup, almost a cliché, that often forces our tears with a small child who stands pale-faced at military attention like John-John Kennedy at Arlington—or more realistically fidgets and pulls at his mother's coat or runs off among the trees. It's understood, and part of the pathos, that the rituals of death as yet mean nothing to this child. But just as often there's an adolescent—a boy in a blue blazer and a borrowed striped tie, a girl in a long cloth coat with a bow in her hair—who's just old enough to comprehend that death is final and serious, and that a familiar emotional landscape has been forever altered.

That was my role, as I recall it, at the first funeral I ever attended. I was thirteen; my great-grandmother, Mary Ann Naylor Crowther, was dead at ninety-four. She was born in Southowram, Yorkshire, near Halifax, during the American Civil War, and immigrated to the United States when she was a girl. She lived in this country for three-quarters of a century and never lost or noticeably altered her mid-Victorian North Country accent. "'Aaarold," she called me, and hated my nickname: "The boy's name is 'Aaarold —'Al's a fool's name." "Name" was pronounced more like "nem," I remember, and she rolled her *L*'s exotically.

I loved my great-grandmother. I was the only great-grandchild old enough to attempt a more or less adult conversation, and old enough to be unintimidated by her strange accent and her great age. She was tall, thin, and ramrod straight, very severe looking when I knew her, but of course she was in her eighties when we met. She was the oldest person I knew. I used to sit up in her room after she broke her hip and could no longer negotiate the stairs. She reminisced about horse-and-buggy England and about Queen Victoria; she claimed to remember the death of Abraham Lincoln, though she was only three when he was killed. We drank tea with milk, a habit I've retained. She indulged me with hard candy, butterscotch and peppermint, from a tin in the top drawer of her dresser. Above the dresser was a Constable-inspired oil painting of an idealized English landscape, a herd of brindle cows in a water meadow at dusk. No doubt my great-grandmother was one of the reasons I gravitated toward the poetry and fiction of Thomas Hardy during my academic period.

My relationship with her was probably the first fully civilized relationship I ever experienced. At her funeral, one of the first questions that came to me was "Who will speak for her now?" She was a domestic spirit from another century who never imposed herself much on the world at large. Though her husband, whom she'd outlived by thirty-three years, had been an ambitious, periodically flamboyant man of business, I've had no luck imagining her as a businessman's wife in the age of George Babbitt. There was much I could never know about her; in her last years no one except me, a child, had been listening to her carefully. And now she was dead.

I suppose it was unusual, along with feeling grief and loss, to be struck as I was by the helplessness of the dead, by their defenselessness as others tell their stories and rank their accomplishments. But I come from a verbal, rhetorical clan, where each of us was perpetually presenting his case and establishing his defense. In one sense I guess everything I've ever written is a part of my brief—my authorized version, to minimize misunderstanding and misinterpretation when I can no longer speak for myself. And I don't deny that I've developed an impulse to speak for others, like my great-grandmother who lived so long and wrote nothing, and said so much less than she should have.

A few years ago I discovered that the dead, even the famous dead, are far more helpless than I had imagined. The dead can't sue, you see, and their descendants can't sue on their behalf. Fools and scoundrels can take a spotless reputation, one that took a century to build, and tear it to shreds before the funeral wreaths have wilted. In a middling gangster movie starring Laurence Fishburne and Tim Roth, I was aghast to find Thomas E. Dewey, the fighting New York DA, governor and near-president of the United States, portrayed as a vile hypocrite and a bagman for the mob. "Can they do that?" I asked a lawyer, and he assured me that they can. Much later I read that some of Dewey's descendants had protested this posthumous smear to no avail.

The dead retain no rights. Too many writers of fiction have discovered that they can attract readers with historical characters—

with expired celebrities. This is a dubious commercial practice, much like rotating TV stars through the casts of Broadway plays, and it proliferates with a reckless disregard for truth or decency. A scene in Guy Vanderhaeghe's novel *The Englishman's Boy* portrays the great actress Lillian Gish as a sloppy, low-rent Hollywood whore. I was enjoying the book, but at this outrage I took personal offense and pitched it across the room. In 1974 I had the privilege of meeting and interviewing Ms. Gish; I was no less charmed by this remarkable woman, then over eighty, than H. L. Mencken had been when he met her in her prime in 1924. "A shrewd, well-informed and amusing woman," the Sage of Baltimore judged her. I found her all of that. And my God, she was wearing a powder-blue wimple, a beautiful woman's last, vain defense against the sad truth that a swan-like neck is not forever. In those days a slave to the movies, I fell half in love with a woman old enough to be my grandmother.

What meanness inspired Vanderhaeghe, one of Canada's better novelists, to commit this sacrilege against history, memory, and, saddest of all, chivalry? Gish had been dead only three years—she lived just short of a century—when he chose to make a dirty joke of her celebrated career. Vanderhaeghe is a writer of actual ability and reputation. Imagine the calumnies the bankable dead can suffer at the hands of pulp writers and hacks.

Fame, fleeting and fragile, is by its nature in the public domain. The mob loves to lift up its idols almost as much as it loves to tear them down. But unless we believe that it all evens out with our just deserts in heaven or hell—I'm not of that persuasion—our mortal reputations deserve more consideration. It isn't right or civilized that you could serve humanity heroically for fifty years—nurse indigents in a barrio, for instance—and yet be dismissed as a drug dealer or a pervert the day after your death by the one malignant enemy you never knew you had. It may sound like a strange cause, and a hopeless one, but there ought to be a law against promiscuous defamation of the dead.

One perceptive reader noted that notable deaths inspired or influenced a fair number of my essays and suggested a diagnosis of chronic, possibly pathological morbidity. In this case I offered no defense. For me an important distinction is that none of these pieces is an obituary. I've written only one assigned obituary in my life, for the soprano who was onstage singing at the Pan-American Exposition in 1901 when Leon Czolgosz assassinated President William McKinley directly in front of her. Interrupted in mid-aria, she climbed down from the stage and tore off strips of her long white concert gown to stanch the dying president's wounds. The rest of her long life—she died in her late nineties—was only slightly less dramatic.

This fortunate assignment from the city desk of the *Buffalo News* opened my eyes to the marvelous possibilities of the form. But an obituary is a deadline assignment, a quick visit to the newspaper's morgue while the deceased still lies in the coroner's. What I've tried to do instead is to reflect at leisure on the context and consequences of certain lives and deaths—lives that affected or intrigued me, in most cases, and lives that were misunderstood or overlooked. Many of the individuals who appear in this book were very well served by their eulogists. At their respective memorial services Marshall Frady was eulogized by Jesse Jackson,

Kirk Varnedoe by the cream of America's art establishment, James Dickey by a chorus of poets, Sister Evelyn Mattern by her peers, some of the loftiest spirits in North Carolina. But others seemed to cry out for a second opinion, a second, more carefully developed petition for posterity's respect. For better or worse, I have frequently served as a self-appointed reputation adjustor, a one-vote final tribunal for the departed.

The adjustment isn't always a positive one. One of the classic adjudicators was Hugh Massingberd (1946–2007), who as obituaries editor of the *Telegraph* of London often bade farewell to his subjects with arch, well-deserved reminders of their least admirable traits and worst humiliations. (Fittingly, the *Telegraph*'s obituary for Massingberd did not omit his gluttony, obesity, or impecuniousness.) Just as the best often need a champion, the dreadful require a stern magistrate when they outlive the public's memory of their crimes. Amnesia blurs and simplifies our heroes and whitewashes most of our villains. My late senator Jesse Helms, neither an intelligent nor a morally evolved individual, offered aid and comfort to South African racists and Central American death squads. Now his disciples want to name buildings after him and clear him to sail across the River Styx in the robes of a statesman. Not on my watch.

The adjustor can't always be kind; he won't always be accurate and definitive either. I've been told that my great admiration for James Dickey's poetry may have softened my portrait of that unmanageable Southern poet. In romanticizing the ethereal Grace Kelly whom I remember singing "True Love" to Bing Crosby in *High Society*, I'm afraid I mourned Princess Grace, after her awful death, as the comforting epitome of a generation of sweet home-loving all-American girls whose like we'll never see again. That was before her biographers revealed a spoiled rich girl of truly unsettling promiscuity. I plead youth on that one, and the youthful infatuation with the movies that I have already confessed. If you have to be wrong about the dead, it's best to err on the side of generosity—an error with which the living have rarely charged me.

My premature canonization of Princess Grace was one of several bursts of misplaced enthusiasm that reminded me of the virtues of the obituary, based on facts and records, as opposed to the eulogy, which blends emotion, memory, and association. These essays, which are neither obituary nor eulogy, aspire to the virtues of both. They represent a sober commitment—no one does this for a living—as well as a great risk that I may be haunted (figuratively or literally) by vengeful shades of the worthy dead I've insulted or shortchanged. As with any altruistic enterprise, whether it's animal rescue or the child-preserver Holden Caulfield lurking in the rye, there's the painful reality that you can't save them all. You're forced to be highly selective. Some lines of poetry that always haunted me are from Eliot's "The Wasteland":

> Unreal City
> Under the brown fog of a winter dawn
> A crowd flowed over London Bridge, so many,
> I had not thought death had undone so many.

Adjustors expect no thanks for our services. But it would be a lie to claim that we seek nothing for ourselves. A journalist strives for clarity, for perspective. Yet the more perspective you achieve, the harder it is to work the daily shift in your profession. Our collective life as a species, viewed from high above, is a succession of wars, skirmishes, and tentative ceasefires among colonies of fierce ants—millennia of chaos and carnage understood imperfectly if at all by the exhausted insects, resolving nothing and defying any interpretation from above. Imposing meaning or a coherent narrative pattern on the actual stuff of our lives is like trying to make sculpture out of water, or so it always seemed to me. Who can shape water unless it's frozen? And death, uniquely, freezes one plane of reality for at least one moment. The face you find on the obituary page belongs to the one sitter who will sit still for his portrait.

A life ended is a story that won't be revised or radically refocused, at least until the historians and biographers begin to chip away at it, and so few of us merit their attention. I can praise or damn the deceased with little fear that the best of them will yet disappoint me, or the worst surprise me. I can hope, in other words, to do justice to them, and offer them confidently as examples.

The other obvious virtue of these churchyard meditations is their inalienable gravity, in which the adjustor selfishly shares. "Death trumps gossip," wrote Larry McMurtry. "Death trumps gab, no matter how brilliant the gabber." Awash in tidal waves of trivia and pop-culture debris, most of us still pause and take off our hats when Death passes; most of us still suspend our self-involvement for sober reflection when Death carries off someone for whom we feel affection or respect. The leveling effect of the mass media, where no one dead or alive is entitled to privacy or dignity, has not yet turned Death into a comic character who waits his turn with the rest.

In Memoriam Thomas Hardy

How to speak with the dead
so that not only
our but their
words are valid?

Unlike their stones,
they scarcely resist us,
memory adjusting
its shades, its mist:

They are too like their photographs
where we can fill
with echoes of our regrets
brown worlds of stillness.

His besetting word
was "afterwards" and it released
their qualities, their restlessness,
as though they heard it.

—Charles Tomlinson

MOLLY IVINS

The Red Rose of Texas

AT THE END of the film *Venus*, which stars Peter O'Toole as a decrepit actor holding off his final curtain, Vanessa Redgrave delivers a bleak line: "When you die, everyone wants to be your friend." Though I knew Molly Ivins forever—since the Kennedy administration—I would never claim that I knew her well. If I implied any special relationship, I'm sure that Molly, listening somewhere, would roll her eyes toward the heavens in one of those gestures of wry exasperation that all of us who knew her scrambled to avoid.

Even in graduate school, during the year at Columbia when I saw her every day, we were nothing approaching inseparable. If she felt I was still struggling with testosterone management, small wonder. At our first meeting, when we were undergraduates in Massachusetts, I was a lamentably unevolved member of one of the more notorious "animal houses" on the Ivy circuit. As irony would have it, a couple of her suitemates at Smith were dating my fraternity brothers. The first time I heard Molly's name they were trying to "fix her up," as we said in those days, with a suitable blind date. Apparently several of these experiments had gone awry; boys had been traumatized. Molly came with more intelligence, sarcasm, and undiluted Texasness than your average New England preppy had ever prepared for, not to mention an unsettling dose of pure height. As I recall it—there are living witnesses to correct my memory and rein in my exaggeration—we found Molly a power forward with a National Merit Scholarship, and still she put him in intensive care.

That some of these experiences might have been painful for Molly, too, was never considered. In spite of our lingering reputation for sissified Aquarian sensitivity, cross-gender empathy was almost unknown among college students of the '6os. There's more than a clue in a column she wrote about her treatment for cancer: "First they mutilate you; then they poison you; then they burn you. I have been on blind dates better than that."

The last time I saw her: Key West, 2004, at a literary seminar celebrating American humor. Mutual friends had been circulating grim rumors about her health. But Molly looked great. She was warm and funny, remembered all the weird characters we had in common, and seemed pleased to see me. After thirty-five years of agreeing with her on nearly every issue, I may, at sixty, have gained a small measure of maturity in her eyes. (Can you tell that it mattered to me?) Thanks to a couple of drinks I was able, even in the inhibiting presence of my wife and other humorists, to tell her how much I'd always appreciated her work and relied on her instincts.

She sipped her mojito. Neither of us cared much for praise close up. But a year later, when I heard she was dying, I was glad I'd taken the risk. The death of a true original attracts a flock of fancy eulogists; everyone from Garrison Keillor to Arianna Huffington has said goodbye to Molly, sharing a wealth of anecdotes and unpublished Mollicisms that I wish I could match. It was a Texas-size sendoff she richly deserved. But her inimitable style and personality, magnified in a media culture that worships personality, sometimes obscured what was most important about Molly Ivins.

Her brand of commentary—intimate, indiscreet, defiantly regional, exuberantly scathing—does not survive her and will not be revisited in the corporatized, gadgetized, homogenized future of print journalism. Like H. L. Mencken, unlike a legion of pinch-faced whiners, Molly leavened her invective with glee. But forget her voice for a moment, if you can—the voice that at its most forceful said, "Listen up, boy, Mama's talkin' to you now" and then dispensed home truths your mother never suspected in language your mother never used. Forget the voice and concentrate on the message. Whenever anyone asked me if there was an indispensable columnist, I'd begin with Molly and sometimes go no further. She was ON MESSAGE, column after column, for twenty years and more, and the message was the one our own Paul Revere would be carrying, if the news still came on horseback—the only message that could possibly save this country from wrack and ruin.

Every week she warned us that our birthright has been sold out from under us, that ruthless, careless corporations and the pluto-crats who profit from them have created a cash-and-carry caricature of democracy. In her own words, which could not be mistaken for anyone else's words: "Oligarchy is eating our ass, our dreams, our country, our heritage, our democracy, our justice, and our tax code."

"Either we figure out how to keep corporate cash out of the po-litical system," she wrote last summer, "or we lose the democracy."

That's all she wrote. It's the only message that matters anymore, and you can stretch it to cover every issue that signifies—the wars, justice, health care, the economy, the environment. While you were watching *American Idol* and playing with your electro-toys, board-room bandits drove away with everything you had. Corporate flun-kies like George Bush ("the master of crony capitalism" —M. I.) and Dick Cheney are not the authors of our misery, any more than Donald Rumsfeld was the author of the cataclysm in Iraq. They're just pieces on the chessboard where macro-capital plays its games, and lightning rods for the occasional outrage those games provoke. If you ever doubted the organic connection between Texas oil poli-tics and the Middle East bloodbath, you never read Molly Ivins.

Her finest hour coincided with the gross polarization and rapid decline of her profession, along with the rise of a belligerent Right Wing that treated mainstream liberals like Marxists. By merely saying what was essential while most of the press labored to ignore it, Molly the prairie populist acquired a radical identity: the Red Rose of Texas, the Lone Star Lady of the Left. Because she was so entertaining, she was even invited on occasion to play that role among the Sunday morning talking heads, on those badminton shows where the political spectrum usually ran from three degrees left of center to three degrees right of Otto von Bismarck. It was proof of her good nature—and incomprehensible to me—that she never, to my knowledge, actually laid hands on Robert Novak or Charles Krauthammer or hurled any heavy objects in their direction. At least nothing heavier than her contempt. The haughty, mean-spirited Krauthammer was always the true acid test of my affections. If you can read four tortured paragraphs of Charles Krauthammer without choking and cursing, you and I would never get along. Molly called him "the ineffable Krauthammer." E-words like "egregious" and "execrable" worked for me.

Molly's solid presence among such people reminded us of their pitiful weightlessness, of the devil's bargain they strike when they hold their places in the Washington food chain by pretending not to see what's clear to a six-year-old—"as obvious as balls on a tall dog," Molly must have said somewhere. The Scooter Libby case is the hilarious quintessence of "The Emperor's New Clothes," performed by the Blind Boys of Foggy Bottom. Did anyone with a fully oxygenated brain ever doubt that the White House (Cheney, Rove, who cares?) tried to burn Joseph Wilson for spoiling their fairy tale about Saddam's awesome arsenal, that they went after him by outing his wife as a CIA agent, that if poor Scooter was the actual leaker he was under orders and set up to take the fall for his boss, probably for future considerations? What part of this was ever unclear? Yet the entire press corps followed Libby's trial as if great truths were being revealed by slow degrees.

Look at the journalists who testified—Novak, Bob Woodward, Tim Russert, Judith Miller—a virtual roll call of Washington's best-connected and most compromised reporters. As Paul Krugman pointed out when Molly died, these were the deep insiders who preserved "highly placed" sources by playing dumb, back when she was warning us that the invasion of Iraq would immortalize George W. Bush as the greatest fool who ever sat in the Oval Office. (History has proven her wrong, but not by elevating W.) And none of them, not even the ones who held his hand in secret, knew Bush half as well as Molly.

When a print journalist of real substance and consequence dies in mid-sentence, so to speak, it's hard in these times to separate her absence from a sense that she was the last of her kind. In Austin in November, Molly herself gave a speech titled "The Future of Journalism, Slow Death or Suicide?" Amid chain-shuffles, sell-offs, layoffs, buyouts of senior staff, and the replacement of columnists by blogs, a wave of retrenchment that almost no dailies have been spared, the American newspaper industry is foundering in plain view. With TV news long gone to the corporate dogs and every solvent magazine scrambling for the key demographics of dumb and nasty, where will the next generation find the free and obstreperous press on which every healthy democracy depends entirely? "Keep these little independent voices alive," was the Ivins prescription. "I think that's where the hope of journalism lies."

Does journalism have a future? Back in the '60s, idealists like Fred Friendly sold it to us as a sacred calling, a kind of priesthood without the celibacy. The answer to what makes a journalist who matters, like Molly Ivins, is the same as the answer to what makes a journalist. Some of our classmates at Columbia had earned under-graduate degrees in journalism; many of them had years of news-room experience. I remember her winking at me once—we were in the same boat, barely legal and stuffed with liberal arts—when some seasoned newsman questioned whether an Ivy League English major was ready to run in the fast lane with real professionals.

Our confidence then was just youthful ignorance, the mother of arrogance. Yet experience never corrected us too severely. The recipe for an effective journalist, then and now, is 1 percent vocational training, 9 percent intelligence, talent, and experience, and 90 percent attitude. The proper attitude? Picture a touchy pit bull who pulls his chain off the ringbolt every time he smells smugness—privilege without humility—and mendacity. A real journalist, we were taught, only unsheathes his pen in the public interest, defending the social contract and protecting the citizen without leverage, the underdog. If you don't believe that, you can write like E. B. White and appear in four hundred newspapers, and you're still a publicist, to me.

Molly Ivins had all the attitude in the world. She blamed it on an overbearing Republican father, a motivation with which I can identify. A world of attitude, and the gloves-off roadhouse prose style to make it stick. It didn't charm everyone. When you die, they all want to be your friends. But they aren't above a patronizing dig or two when you're no longer there to defend yourself. I don't know that "loneliness" plagued Molly any more than it plagues most intelligent people. I thought a line about her "battle" with alcohol was gratuitous and naive. You don't "battle" alcohol the way you battle cancer. Alcohol isn't your enemy—it's an old friend you can never trust but with whom you share many of your sweetest memories. Reporters who never drank were very rare in the newsrooms of yore, and of low prestige.

One posthumous critic thought Molly's Calamity Jane persona, the one that hollered "Let's rodeo!" to motivate a gathering of left-wing reporters, was a touch disingenuous for an upper-middle class girl who went to Smith. But which of us educated exiles from the provinces (in the media, everywhere but the East Coast and LA) hasn't amped up the old accent when someone from home walked into the room? Molly had to earn her spurs in Texas before she tackled the rest of the country, and Texas is a hazardous high-testosterone zone where a woman has to be a little larger than life to command some attention. If she had detractors, I suspect they were grandsons of the old boys who condescended to the great Dorothy Parker.

As Regina Barreca wrote in Parker's defense, "It's not hard to dream up a conspiracy plot which demands that all women writers who speak successfully with a satirical tongue get lacerated critically, or, worse, that such women are presented as sad, shriveled shells of frivolous femininity, or—worse still, worst ever—that women who don't act nicely *get left alone.*"

Amen. A lot of men carry secret grudges against women who don't make them feel smarter and taller. Molly Ivins could operate with Dorothy Parker's scalpel, but she also packed a chainsaw in her toolbox, which cleared the way for the coarser chainsaw journalism of women like Maureen Dowd of the *New York Times*. These editors who encourage Dowd might even have been able to accommodate Molly, but it was an appalling mismatch when she went to work for the *Times* in 1976. Encouraged by "legendary" editors who could never write a lick (Abe Rosenthal gets a century in pressroom purgatory for assigning Molly Ivins to City Hall), the tradition at the *Times* was to crush—to neuter—any writer who betrayed the slightest pleasure in manipulating the English language. Molly's six years there must have seemed like forty.

Unfortunately she was a few years ahead of the *Times*, and ahead of her time. But she was a big girl who didn't need the likes of me to stick up for her, then or now. My only quarrel with Molly Ivins was philosophical. She always claimed that she was an incurable optimist; I tend to swing the other way. Scrape away a few layers of accumulated irony and I'm not so different from another of our contemporaries, songwriter Joni Mitchell, who says, "My heart is broken in the face of the stupidity of my species." I followed David Broder once on a public radio show. When the host told me that the tirelessly sanguine Broder had just proclaimed his great faith in the American people, I replied, "In my experience, anyone who praises the wisdom of the people is trying to get away with something."

I like to think that Molly wouldn't shout me down on that one. If she declared that Texas legislators were dumber than houseplants and root vegetables, she must have considered the intelligence of the people who voted for them. One of her last columns noted the difference between populists, who are born with the ability to recognize their friends and their enemies, and the liberals who like to split hairs and set traps for each other. She was never an ideologue, of course, but a one-of-a-kind, organic, hands-on populist. As I see it, it was never the wisdom but the ornery, dirt-plain humanity of people that won her heart. And it was probably a much bigger heart, to begin with, than most of us ever brought to the newsroom.

JOHN HOPE FRANKLIN

A Long View, Unsweetened

FOR MOST OF America's four centuries as concept, colony, and constitutional republic, African-Americans played small roles in its recorded history and a much smaller role in recording it. In the few decades since that began to change, there have been false starts and poor players who mounted the stage to strut and fret. One school of defiant black historians set about revising history to please black America, turning ancient Hebrews, Egyptians, and every non-Aryan people never actually photographed into proto-Africans. Considering the millennia during which Africans were invisible to Western historians, this seemed fair enough—but not quite true enough. Much worse, educated African-Americans like Clarence Thomas exploited new opportunities for high office and civic distinction by revising reality to please white America.

Historian John Hope Franklin, a North Carolina state treasure who died in Durham at the age of ninety-four, was the ageless antidote to all that. Franklin deplored Clarence Thomas and cited his dismal mismanagement of the Equal Employment Opportunity Commission as one of the gross racial failures of the Reagan administration. He wrote in the *New York Times* that Thomas's confirmation "bleached white" the Supreme Court's "Negro" seat so long and honorably occupied by Thurgood Marshall. Without pandering to any constituency, Franklin made his way against the longest odds that confronted any scholar of his generation. Beginning in the 1930s he wrote America's story as he saw it, whether or not it pleased his readers. His candor was sometimes unsettling, not only to those who harbored traditional prejudices but to every meliorist and mediocrity who only wanted to make nice. Awarding Dr. Franklin the Presidential Medal of Freedom in 1995, Bill Clinton—one of the few presidents we'd ever suspect of actually reading his books—testified to Franklin's notorious independence: "He looks history straight in the face and tells it like it is."

Plain speaking and unsweetened history create misunderstandings. There are still white people who prefer their distinguished African-Americans with a dash of cheerful amnesia. An asset to diplomats but a deadly poison to historians, amnesia was one thing John Hope Franklin never suffered and never offered. A local academic mandarin, white, of course, but with the best liberal credentials, told me that he'd never met Franklin but heard he was "a little bitter." I recommended Franklin's autobiography, *Mirror to America* (2005). You need only read to the fourth paragraph to find a chilling litany of the worst humiliations and malignancies the historian endured in what he calls "the race jungle" of twentieth-century America. It begins with his eviction from a segregated railroad coach at the age of six and concludes with a dreadful piece of idiocy at a private club in Washington, DC, where the eighty-year-old Franklin, a member, is mistaken for the coat-check attendant by a white member's wife. (The obtuseness of this woman verges on the spectacular since Dr. Franklin was famously well tailored; he dressed in public like an ambassador, in suits that would cost a coat-check attendant six months' salary.) Also on his list of afflictions were the race riot in Tulsa that burned his father's law office, a Mississippi mob that threatened to lynch him, a gifted brother driven to what appears to have been suicide by his mistreatment in the U.S. Army, and a blind woman who refused to let the twelve-year-old Franklin help her to cross the street when she realized that he was not a white boy. He called these "everyday, ordinary experiences" and acknowledged that contemporaries without his advantages suffered far worse.

"In my early years," Franklin wrote in *Mirror to America*, "there was never a moment in any contact with white people that I was not reminded that society as a whole had sentenced me to abject humiliation for the sole reason that I was not white."

Possibly "bitter" is a word that empathy-challenged white people should not use carelessly. African-American history, often unbearable and always inconvenient, is the huge sore place in the national memory that helps to keep us honest and humble. At times, on both sides of the racial barrier, there's an unseemly impatience to forget what Franklin remembered. He was not only one of the last scholars but one of the last witnesses from his generation; as such he bore the heavy responsibility of remembering for others. But the burden of memory never made him the kind of individual that "bitter" might suggest. A tall man of unforced dignity, Franklin was always courtly and affable, with a sly grin and an impish wit he unleashed in company he trusted. Pressed to describe his manner, I'd say that it was the precise opposite of the merry, light-minded obsequiousness once expected of African-Americans when white people were in the room. Whether he was born with this watchful gravitas or, as a preternaturally keen observer, crafted it carefully over the decades, I never knew him well enough to say.

I was proud to know him at all. Though the pleasure of his company was considerable, it was usually reserved for a fortunate few. One admirer who attempted to correct that was Tim Tyson, author of *Blood Done Sign My Name*, who persuaded Franklin to appear in a cameo role in the motion picture version of his book, filmed in North Carolina in 2008. In his acting debut, at ninety-three, the historian played an elderly gentleman who shows a group of young men how to calm a difficult mule and load it on a truck. The symbolism is appropriate—what mule was ever more muleheaded than the white population of the rural South?—and Tyson explained that he wanted Franklin for "his dignity and intelligence," and to make the point "that there were black people of that generation who worked mules but could have been United States senators." Not coincidentally, Tyson's critically acclaimed book chronicled an unpunished racist murder in Oxford, NC, in 1970 that historians list as one of the last of the South's lynch-style atrocities.

If you saw the film, you met a man who never doubted his ability to charm people, yet made a career of his ability to discomfit them. Though his most influential book was *From Slavery to Freedom: A History of Negro Americans* (published in 1947, the year Jackie Robinson arrived in Brooklyn), Franklin always objected when he was described as a scholar of African-American history. He wrote *American* history, he insisted, but with the deleted parts restored: "For much of my career, what I have been trying to do is correct American history. I've not been trying to create a field. I've been trying to fill in what has been systematically left out." To wall off historians as African-Americanists, Franklin argued, was just an academic form of segregation.

The deleted history he restored can be relentlessly depressing. For publication in 1963, the centennial of the Emancipation Proclamation, the United States Commission on Civil Rights engaged Dr. Franklin to write an official history of civil rights in America. The one he submitted was not favorably received in Washington. They had hoped for an upbeat celebration of the achievements of black Americans—the standard social studies version we were all served in grade school, with George Washington Carver tinkering in his peanut laboratory and Booker T. Washington declaiming in his classroom, and all the rest whitewash. Franklin had written, instead, a balanced history that called attention to the crimes and indecencies committed against black people and the barriers that had made their achievements so difficult. To the commission's request for "a note of greater tolerance and moderation," Franklin replied,

"The history of the Negro and civil rights in the United States is not a pretty picture." The final much-edited and adulterated version was a sour disappointment for him, though no surprise. "Of the many instances in which it appeared that I was used by the United States government," Franklin records in his autobiography, "this is the clearest, most unequivocal example."

Far from sugarcoating the wretched history of race relations, Franklin relished the most excruciating ironies. Bill Clinton's favorite John Hope Franklin story was a kind of *Twilight Zone* train ride the historian took from Greensboro to Durham, NC, in 1945. A half coach was overcrowded with black passengers while a full coach carried just six white men. The conductor, bound by Jim Crow laws of the day, refused to switch the coaches or redistribute the passengers—even though the six white men were German prisoners of war. Nor did Franklin's taste for irony spare the academy and the politically correct. At Duke, where he had taught since 1982, he was a wry observer of the school's controversial effort to leapfrog over the Ivy League with the most cutting-edge English faculty in captivity. A key recruit was Henry Louis Gates, Jr., the noted African-American literary scholar, and the chief recruiter was English Department chairman Stanley Fish. Fish honored Gates at an unfortunate luncheon to which he invited only black faculty—and then took his leave, so that Gates found himself dining in a segregated lunchroom. Franklin's delight in this gaffe, related in loving detail in *Mirror to America*, may have brought a blush to the cheek of the self-possessed Fish, an acquaintance of mine who is famously hard to embarrass.

The Fish story reminds us how easily the most sophisticated

and well-meaning white liberal can stumble into interracial quicksand. Among white historians, the late, illustrious Vann Woodward was one of Franklin's oldest friends and supporters. But they
were briefly estranged when Woodward, like most scholars of his
generation skeptical of race-and-gender academic fashions, wrote
a semi-favorable review of a book by the egregious right-wing critic
Dinesh D'Souza—who in his attack on Duke and other liberaliz-
ing universities appeared to include Franklin's appointment as part
of a wave of affirmative action. Franklin responded indignantly in
a letter to the *New York Review of Books*. The old friends patched
it up, but after Woodward's death Franklin wrote, "Vann and I
necessarily viewed the world through different lenses, felt nuances
with different degrees of acuity. If he viewed the Civil Rights Act
and the Voting Rights Act as signal victories, to me they were tenu-
ous toeholds that could slip away at any moment, as indeed they
seemed to be doing even as we exchanged letters."

Franklin's autobiography is a life lesson in the critical nuances
that separate the white liberal optimist from the wary black re-
alist with traumatic memories. Unlike so many memoirs, *Mirror to America* doesn't shout, "Look at me and what I've accom-
plished," but "Look at me and ask yourself why there aren't a
hell of a lot more like me." From where Franklin sat, white self-
congratulation is always aggravating, and "measurable progress"
for African-Americans, 150 years after the Fourteenth and Fif-
teenth Amendments, was no occasion for applause. Where Woodward saw victories, Franklin saw small, hard-won concessions to
justice, long overdue. The man who witnessed the rejection, persecution, and ultimate exile of many of the twentieth century's brav-

est and proudest black Americans—Jack Johnson, Paul Robeson, James Baldwin, and W. E. B. Du Bois (whom Franklin knew well), to name just a few—was disinclined to applaud America's passionate embrace of an Oprah Winfrey or Tiger Woods. Black celebrities, he argued, are just anecdotes that distract us from abandoned neighborhoods, resegregated public schools, and the shocking percentages of young black males who are imprisoned or unemployed.

A reporter once asked Franklin, in his ninetieth year, if he was optimistic about race relations in America. "No, I don't think it's necessary," he answered. "If there is really no basis, if it's a blind optimism, that only delays recognition of the problems that must be fixed."

The ingrained pessimism of black intellectuals, which is sometimes converted to careless rhetoric, has been dismissed as political correctness by whites of the happy-face persuasion. Reading Franklin carefully shows how much deeper and darker it runs. He never denied positive change: "Of course the racial picture has been radically modified," he wrote. "Much has remained unchanged, but certainly in the twentieth century we saw tremendous legal gains, changes that created the structure, if not the will, for equality." He only denied, compellingly, that there was a positive balance or a positive trend.

"The victories of the civil rights era did not wipe away three centuries of slavery, degradation, segregation, and discrimination," Franklin wrote. "What does the fact that in 2001 there were more young black men in jails and penitentiaries than in college say for the direction in which our society is moving?"

These assessments were made, of course, before anyone suspected that Barack Obama, not precisely an "African-American" but at least an "African/American," a person of color, would be elected president in 2008. I was particularly touched by Franklin's memory of his optimistic parents, who "taught me to believe that I could be, as they then articulated it, the first Negro president of the United States." As a young man, he recalled, he often declared his White House ambitions with "tongue in cheek." Though his parents never came close to casting their votes for the first black president, Dr. Franklin, in his tenth decade, fulfilled their dream. On the morning of November 5, 2008, he must have read the headlines with that shrewd, ageless grin we all remember. I'd have paid a pretty penny to have been there.

FATHER THOMAS BERRY

Deep Greens and Blues

WHY DO IMPORTANT writers fail to receive the recognition they deserve? Ask a serious reader today, and he's likely to roll his eyes at you, the answer is so obvious. Too few Americans still read, in any serious way, and too few hard-pressed publishers will take a chance on an interesting writer who may not sell. A smug sub-literacy is spreading like dense fog across America's cerebral landscape; when and how it might clear, no one I know is prepared to say. But the question of neglected writers used to be much more complicated.

The death in June 2009 of the Rev. Thomas Berry, C.P., was a great loss to the literary, theological, and environmental communities, and to me personally as an admirer and retailer of his ideas. Father Berry, a cultural historian who called himself a "geologian," was arguably the most significant writer of nonfiction the Carolinas produced in the twentieth century. Though his death at ninety-four was hardly premature or unanticipated, I mourned him with a trace of guilt. Berry lived his last years and died in Greensboro, where he was born and raised. Though he was a citizen of the world who lived in China, Germany, and the Philippines at different points in his career, he was, in a way important to him, a Tar Heel. For a decade I served on a committee that recommends candidates for the North Carolina Awards to the governor. Literary candidates were my particular concern. It was only when he died that I realized no one had ever nominated Berry for this honor, reserved for distinguished North Carolina natives and residents. I never thought to short-list him, either, even though I was reading his books—even though one of his nieces is a friend of mine.

It's no excuse, but Berry enjoyed much wider recognition in New York and in Europe, where I met several disciples of his deep-Green theology, than he ever did in the state where he was born. Among his many honorary degrees, only one, from Elon University when he was ninety-three, was awarded by a school in North Carolina. On reflection, this is not so surprising. If he'd received his medal and ribbon from our governor, as he should have many years ago, Berry would have been honored with a group that nearly always includes a representative of one of the tobacco or textile fortunes that provide the lion's share of North Carolina's sustaining philanthropy, not to mention its political contributions. A cautious governor might have hesitated to embrace the scholar-priest who wrote, in *The Dream of the Earth*, of our "instinctive awareness that the corporation is in the business of seducing the consumer while plundering natural resources and poisoning the environment"— and specifically listed Burlington Mills as one of the evil giants of the industrial/technological age he so eloquently detested.

He was a radical, this soft-spoken, grandfatherly priest who spent his twenties, those years when most of us run as wild as we're able, in a Passionist monastery. His special status as a Catholic priest made him a marked minority figure in the Protestant Bible Belt and meant that his public profile depended to some extent on the support of his church. Yet Berry, whose fundamental argument was that arrogant humanity has overrun and devastated this sweet planet, forfeited Catholic sympathy by criticizing the church's positions on population control. He himself was the third of thirteen children. "It's here that religion has been at fault," he said of the population bomb. "Especially the Catholic religion—which has failed extensively in not paying attention to the decline of the natural world." In an interview with poet and nature writer John Lane, Father Berry, at ninety-one, called for a clean sweep of the establishment: "We need new religions. We need new laws. New economics and new education. All four."

Like the French Jesuit Pierre Teilhard de Chardin, whose ideas influenced him profoundly, Thomas Berry became a theological embarrassment to Catholic superiors who would have preferred that he not publish at all. (Unlike Teilhard, whose subversive theology was only published posthumously, Berry was never directly censored by the Vatican.) If he failed to get his due from the civic and academic establishments in North Carolina, that was no disappointment to the Catholic Church. Each of us who trouble the world with our opinions has consoled himself, at one time or another, with Matthew 13:57, "A prophet is not without honor, save in his own country." But it's a rare case like Berry's where we're speaking of an actual prophet. His church used to burn original thinkers; even now such thinkers find no intellectual homeplace, no true community except the one they form with kindred spirits. Berry's compensation for the honors we denied him was the greatest compensation any writer can receive, the certain knowledge that he was right. And the stoic pleasure—though perhaps Father Berry was above it—of watching his enemies and detractors, the ones who were wrong, receding in history's rearview mirror.

Few writers have been so right so often as Thomas Berry. If you're unfamiliar with his work, it's not merely his English prose that sets him apart, though that prose is precise and often poetic, rich in aphorisms and flexible in a way you might expect from a polymath and linguist whose command of languages included Chinese and Sanskrit. What Berry was able to do, from his position outside or at least at the margin of an imprisoning commercial society, was to see the wide world and its troubled history with alarming clarity. He had satellite vision. In comparison to most of his twentieth-century contemporaries, it was a vision that elevated him like an eagle among burrowing rodents.

Any reader with a Green heart has encountered some of the themes and language of deep ecology, the radical environmental movement that embraces Berry as one of its gurus and prophets. Though some of its connections are extremely subtle, the main thrust of its argument is not. "The ultimate source of evil in the existing order of life is its commitment to human well-being at the expense of the natural world," Berry wrote. The druids of deep ecology teach that the earth is a sacred single organism that includes humanity. It will only survive, and we as an integral part of it can only survive, if we acknowledge our interdependence with all creation and alter our geocidal, suicidal behavior accordingly. "Spiritual autism" is Berry's term for our fatal deafness, the obliviousness to all nonhuman needs and rights that saps the planet's lifeblood and brings its ecosystems to the verge of catastrophic collapse. And the hour is very late. In *The Dream of the Earth*, written more than thirty years ago, Berry warned, "We are indeed closing down the major life systems of the planet."

"We are saturating the air, the water, and the soil with toxic substances so that we can never bring them back to their original purity," he continued. "We are upsetting the entire earth system that has, over some billions of years and through an endless sequence of experiments, produced such a magnificent array of living forms, forms capable of seasonal self-renewal over an indefinite period of time."

Berry's warning is in the language of actual, physical apocalypse, far from the Christians' psychedelic apocalypse in the book of Revelation. He calls the fatal disconnection between humans and the natural world "the supreme pathology," a chronic psychosis that approaches its breaking point in the "radically anthropocentric" culture of the West, where industrial capitalism, technological intoxication, and a demonic myth of progress have brought us, in his words, "to wasteworld instead of wonderworld."

From conservative Greensboro, downwind from the cigarette factories of Winston-Salem, in the very shadow of Burlington Mills, came this Jeremiah, this Ezekiel proclaiming bad news, not for miscreant Hebrews but for all the sinful tribes of man. Berry traced his Green philosophy, a lifelong commitment to the defense of the earth, to a single visionary moment when he was eleven, in a meadow full of lilies and wildflowers near his parents' home. "Whatever preserves and enhances this meadow in the natural cycles of its transformation is good," he decided. "What is opposed to this meadow or negates it is not good."

Berry always had much to say that no one wanted to hear—no one, that is, except the troubled few of us who view each day's cultural phenomena with bewilderment and dismay and desperately seek a sane voice among the chorus of mad ones. At times he was hauntingly prescient. Writing in the mid-'80s, before computers were personal, back when cell phones were experiments instead of electronic leeches fastened permanently to every human body, Berry deplored the cyber-obsession that has, in the few years since, completely altered the human equation and exponentially widened the fatal gap between wired humanity and the natural world. "We can invent computers capable of processing ten million calculations per second," he wrote (is that slow now?). "And why? To increase the volume and the speed with which we move natural resources through the consumer economy to the junk pile or the waste heap." He speculated, as I have, on the evolutionary fate of a species featuring hardwired immobile children living virtual lives. Years later, in his interview with John Lane, Berry cited with disgust a study claiming that 70 percent of America's children are now overweight.

More American universities might have chosen to honor him if Berry's dismissal of corporate-subsidized higher education had been less thorough. "This alienation from the earth venture has led to confusion about the entire human venture; the college has no adequate context in which to function," he declared, and consequently it turns out docile supplicants for corporate bounty instead of articulate citizen-critics of a corporate culture that devours the earth. His harsh view of the academy was amplified by the more acerbic Wendell Berry (kindred but no kin), who calls these specialized graduates "itinerant professional vandals" and "a race of learned mincers, whose propriety and pride is to keep their minds inside their 'fields,' as if human thoughts were a kind of livestock to be kept out of the woods and off the roads."

The beauty of Thomas Berry's books, and his vision, is that there is always a compelling story line, a unified narrative from which his opinions emerge organically. Unlike the conventional, feverish prophet of doom, he takes the long, long view, and takes his time. There are few comprehensive critiques of the human enterprise that fit together as seamlessly as this restless Southern priest's. One resonant story line, which he calls "Patriarchy: A New Interpretation of History," begins with the emergence of a particularly phallocentric Bronze Age tribe, the Hebrews, who injected Western history with a poisonous dose of testosterone from which it has never recovered. The teachings of Jesus Christ may have mitigated the machismo, but Jesus was a Jew after all, and the vain, vindictive Yahweh who bullies his way through the Old Testament remains a grim presence in Judeo-Christian theology and the cultures it created. Wars, tyranny, nationalism, the subjugation of women and other races, and a cruel, rigid church that purported to represent Jesus were logical consequences of the triumph of the male principle over the female, in Berry's scenario. But it was the hyperphallic modern era of heavy industry, bellicose capitalism, and space-age technology that polluted the earth and drained its resources so rapidly, and set the West's testosterone-fueled juggernaut on the final fast road to planetary destruction.

What I love most about this story is the way it sets the table for a wonderfully subversive heresy, more threatening to Catholic and Christian orthodoxy than any of the pantheist speculations of Teilhard de Chardin. By creating a man-god, in the double sense of species and gender, Western man betrayed his foolish narcissism—wouldn't any creature with the need and imagination to create a deity create it in his own image, wouldn't a planet of sentient rats worship a rat-god? But this man also turned away from his Mother Earth, the goddess Gaia or Gaea whom the Greeks adapted from earlier, gynocentric religions that predated the Hebrew bible. And the rest is history, as Berry has explained, with the end of history looming as geocide—as matricide. The theology he implies, without stating it bluntly, is the apotheosis of pantheism. God didn't make the world, (S)he *is* the world, waiting for the worship (S)he deserves. Our deity, our salvation, and our identity are all right here in this created and creative universe, above our heads, beneath our feet. And in our bones—we can't escape God because we're part of God, like everything else in Nature. (No one captures the pantheist epiphany quite as lyrically as Teilhard de Chardin: "The most we can say is that at certain times a wind greater than we, coming we know not whence, passes through our soul.")

In one deft stroke, Berry scandalizes fundamentalists, makes traditional religions sound primitive and sophomoric, and undercuts atheism, which in this light appears tone-deaf and simplistic. Human beings have been listening in vain for the man-voice from the sky, some with endless hope, some turning away in disgust, while the earth was speaking to us constantly in a thousand voices, the loudest one crying "Stop!" and "Help!" In this same turn, Berry effectively demonizes the Western "economy of plunder." The pantheist conclusion is that anyone who harms the earth attacks God personally, committing the unpardonable sacrilege. As an amateur theologian, I'm dumb with admiration for what Berry has wrought here. I heard a Unitarian minister describe a "new Unitarian spirituality" that's spreading in his church. It sounds precisely like the radiant pantheism of the Catholic druid from Greensboro.

A prophet's voice is silenced, after nearly a century of eloquent dissent. Though it continues to echo, notably in two books of his essays—*The Sacred Universe* and *The Christian Future and the Fate of the Earth*—that were published after his death. Their readers, and I hope there are many, will quickly grasp one more thing about Father Berry that amazed me. Like many men of the cloth he was, for all the dark knowledge he accumulated, an incurable optimist. The hour is late, the damage is dreadful, and so are the selfishness and ignorance that conspire to compound it. Only idiots deny the rapid, lethal advance of global warming. But Berry died believing in the dawn of a new consciousness, the imminence of an Ecozoic Age—Pax Gaia—where a generation of enlightened humans will stifle the old devils and rescue the earth from the brink of oblivion.

He still believed in us. We are very sick, and this was one physician whose diagnosis was always dead on. For the accuracy of his prognosis, we can only pray.

LANCE CORPORAL
BRIAN ANDERSON

A Farewell to Arms

T HE RISING SUN is just clearing the ridge behind me, lighting
up weeping cherry trees in peerless full bloom. A fresh breeze
carries the dense, sweet scent of wisteria down the terraces to
the bench where I read my newspaper. So far I'm the only Sunday
pilgrim in the Sarah P. Duke Gardens—which every April make
their powerful plea for the tarnished soul of old Buck Duke, the
tobacco baron whose vast fortune built the university, the hospital,
and the chapel that tower over this vernal splendor.

It's the first morning of daylight saving, the first Sunday and first clear, perfect day of the cruelest month, and here in the Eden that Buck built, it will be a blessed hour before tourists and photographers begin to cluster around the koi pond and the weeping cherries. I'm acutely aware of my good fortune. In Iraq, friends and former colleagues are chewing sand and ducking bullets in 100-degree temperatures. Tomorrow morning, one of them will dominate the obituary page of the *New York Times*. But it's the local paper that I'm reading, and I see that the second headline—after "Siege of Baghdad begins"—honors a local Marine, Lance Corporal Brian Anderson, killed Wednesday in the desert west of Nasiriyah.

"Marine 'gave his life for the rest of us,'" it reads, quoting Cpl. Anderson's mother. This wasn't a classic death like the ones Marines die in John Wayne movies, cut down in firefights against impossible odds. The corporal, operating a .50-caliber machine gun atop a seven-ton truck, was electrocuted when the truck rolled through some low-hanging power lines.

Anderson was born and raised here in Durham, NC. Though he lived within a mile of campus, the cloistered, expensive world of Duke University would have been as remote from his experience as Baghdad. He played football, ran track, and wrestled at Riverside High School, sang in the choir and played conga drums at Mount Calvary United Church of Christ. He enlisted in the Marines shortly after his high school graduation in 1996, "probably trying to find himself," said a family friend.

According to his mother, Anderson planned to re-enlist and was hoping to learn computers. His friends described him as popular and easygoing, his potential beyond the Marine Corps largely unexplored. His official photograph in the Corps's striking dress uniform suggests a confident young man who had found a home and a focus at Camp Lejeune.

Anderson's is a representative portrait from the professional, all-volunteer armed forces that are fighting America's wars—and a fairly typical profile of the Southern warrior, circa 2003. It's here in the South, particularly in North Carolina with its sprawling bases and military economy, that virtually any war is embraced with enthusiasm. If the president declared war on Quebec—even on South Carolina—he could expect Tar Heels to give him the same 75 percent approval that greeted his "liberation" of Iraq.

If you've never seen a three-year-old dressed in camo and a Special Forces beret, try a gun show in Raleigh. Ours is a martial province, bounded on the south by Georgia where they've been hammering out a compromise on the Confederate battle flag, on the north by Virginia where Richmond troglodytes have been fighting a rear-guard action against Daniel French's statue of Abraham Lincoln. Liberals who liked the cut of North Carolina's senior senator, presidential candidate John Edwards, were stunned to discover that he was a firm supporter of the Baghdad adventure. (The first of several stunning discoveries about Sen. Edwards.) They didn't understand that any other position would eliminate his political influence in North Carolina, forever.

Among Tar Heels, "supporting the troops" seems to mean a good deal more than praying for their safe return. Very little changes here, from war to war—except the young people in uniform and the families that produce them. It's a substantial irony, lost on many "supporters" of the late Cpl. Anderson, that Abraham Lincoln's war won Anderson and other African-Americans their right to wear the gorgeous dress uniform of the United States Marines. There are star-spangled, pennant-waving white people here and elsewhere whose passions for the armed forces and for college basketball—roughly equal—are untempered by the fact that their own children no longer participate.

Just as coaches at the South's mostly white universities earn millions exploiting black players from urban ghettoes, white generals from West Point earn their stars on the backs of men like Brian Anderson. As an athlete he wasn't good enough for Duke, for the crosstown bus ride to glory that was the impossible dream of nearly every kid in his neighborhood. But he was good enough for the Marines, good enough to fight in the desert and die in one of the most dubious wars Americans have ever tried to justify.

A volunteer army is a poor people's army. Anderson was a child of privilege compared to Lance Corporal Jose Gutierrez, another Marine who died in combat south of Baghdad. Gutierrez was an orphan from Guatemala who crossed the Mexican-American border illegally, at fourteen. He joined the Marine Corps as an immigrant foreign national, but through the infinite generosity of the immigration bureau, he was naturalized posthumously and buried as a United States citizen.

Casualty reports, like Division I basketball teams, rarely include middle-class white kids anymore—a fact legions of war lovers have agreed to ignore. Avoiding military service is as easy as getting into college, and these days that's a pretty low hurdle to clear. This class exemption is hard to take when it's personified by smug sophomores whose exposure to real-life violence consists of fraternity hazing and post-tournament riots. It's impossible to take when they express enthusiasm for wars of Arab liberation. A friend of mine, a professor at Wake Forest University, had one student who objected strenuously to antiwar sentiments she expressed in class.

"I respect your right to choose," she told him. "I guess this means you'll drop out of school and enlist." As she tells it, the war weasel recoiled as if he'd been stung by a hornet.

Iraq is a surrogate's war fought by the children of an economic underclass, a remote war compared to a struggle for national survival like World War II, when Rose Kennedy's sons took the same risks as her chauffeur. A cynical war of geopolitical chess, it seems unworthy of patriotic posturing. (If you want to keep the enemy in check, Henry Kissinger would say, you have to sacrifice a few pawns.) This is a war in which only the most hypocritical propagandist—or the most heartbroken mother—could claim that a fallen Marine "gave his life for the rest of us." Yet the life he gave is no less precious, whether the Marine's enemy is Adolf Hitler or some grotesque, well-oiled dictator who fell out with old friends in the U.S. State Department. In a time of sordid little wars with suspicious agendas, how does the martial South keep faith with its warriors?

Do we call Cpl. Anderson a hero, a martyr, an innocent victim? On the surface he was just a young man in search of direction, self-discipline, and self-respect. The Marine Corps is the last place I would have looked for them myself—if you remember the fat, humiliated recruit in Stanley Kubrick's *Full Metal Jacket*, the one who ultimately kills his drill instructor and himself, he's the character in war films with whom I most closely identify. But I've known too many Marines to doubt that the Corps delivers most of what it promises in the line of pride and self-respect. Right up to the instant when he hit the power lines, Anderson must have thought he'd struck a fine bargain with the U.S. Marines.

It's fraught with such complexity, this business of "supporting our troops." Antiwar extremists made a fatal error when they stigmatized soldiers for the debacle in Vietnam—an error that never tempted me because my brother was serving in a forward unit. But consider the current right-wing rhetoric, insisting that a patriot drops every objection to military action once U.S. forces are committed. This is moral quicksand, a mindless lemming-rush to moral suicide. Followed to its logical conclusion, it outlaws individual conscience and mandates unanimous civilian support for every bellicose tyrant from Hitler to Idi Amin—or Saddam Hussein.

We honor our soldiers by separating the reasons they're in Iraq—because military risk falls unequally on minorities and the poor, because U.S. foreign policy is turning toxic, because a paranoid America is turning mean and ugly since 9-11-01—from the irreducible fact that they are there, where we have no right to send them unless we'd gladly fight alongside them. Cpl. Anderson was there, and his Durham neighbors in the Duke-blue sweaters were not. I can call him a hero, not because he died defending American ideals (he died obeying masters who flout them), but because he died defending his fellow Marines, exposed in a conflict they did not cause or seek.

The face of war has changed immeasurably since Lee and Longstreet sat by their campfire at Gettysburg; war as it touches individuals is always the same. Pure pacifists say we must never praise soldiers because the wars will never end until all the world's young men (and now women) refuse to serve. Until then—until, perhaps, the end of time—we rely on Cpl. Anderson. I don't feel compromised, as an incorrigible war-hater, when I say that I'm proud of him. I'm equally proud of the ragged band of war protesters I encountered at the University of Virginia, marching soaked in freezing rain, herded by contemptuous police, carrying the homemade banner "Regime Change Begins at Home." Like me, their support for Cpl. Anderson consisted of fervent, unanswered prayers for his safe return. Though gulfs of circumstance and misunderstanding still separate them, it's a noble dream that someday the warriors of conscience and the warriors of necessity will march on common ground.

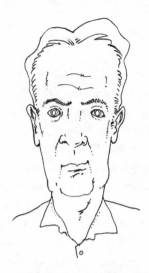

JAMES DICKEY

The Last Wolverine

A T HIS MEMORIAL service, they all said he was bigger than life. He was definitely bigger than me. For a prosemonger, I seem to have met a host of poets; James Dickey was the only one who ever clamped me in a headlock I couldn't break.

It was a cruel introduction to genius. Dickey was my literary idol. His poetry, beginning with the publication of "May Day Sermon to the Women of Gilmer County, Georgia, by a Woman Preacher Leaving the Baptist Church," broke a grade-school spell cast by T. S. Eliot and bloodless sages writing dirges in the dark, sipping weak tea, and waiting for the end.

Dickey raged up out of Georgia like an unstable air mass, a sudden storm that blows the windows open. "Class dismissed," snarled those outlaw bikers, bullwhip Baptists, and carnivorous mammals who stalked his violent verse. When life was all possibility and poetry seemed indispensable, *Poems, 1957–1967* was my Bible. I still own the original paperback, that thick green volume with the cherubic Dickey on the cover, in his button-down shirt and tie. Nearly every page is separated from the binding now, and half of them are stained with red wine, which I know he'd appreciate.

I met the poet in 1969, in the prime of his career. I'd organized a poetry contest for employees of Time, Inc. Someone at *Life* talked Dickey into judging the finalists and flying up to New York to grace the presentations. I was awed at the prospect of meeting him and delighted with his choices—third prize for my girlfriend and first prize to *Time* proofreader Susan Mitchell, who submitted a remarkable poem (she was later a finalist for the National Book Award in poetry).

Joy reigned through Dickey's reading of Susan's poem. I wanted those New Yorkers to hear a true poet read in the drawl they associated with George Wallace and Lester Maddox. Dickey was superb, but I noticed that his bottle of Jack Daniel's was half empty. The whiskey was below the label when he said something sexually explicit—menacing, actually—to the prizewinner; the bottle was empty when he seized me in a headlock that all but turned out my lights.

When Dickey lost interest in killing me, I lurched free and noticed that the editors and executives had left the reception. My story gets worse, in some ways, but the gory details are generic. A lot of poetry lovers were tested by these performances. Nearly twenty years later I worked up the courage to remind him of our first encounter. The only thing Dickey could remember was Susan Mitchell's poem.

It was Dickey who established, at least for the Southern circuit, the notorious *droit d'écrivain*—the unwritten law that for all women who attend literary events, the sexual claims of a visiting writer take precedence over any previous relationships, including marriage. He seemed honestly, innocently surprised when a woman or her escort failed to recognize his claim. At one women's college they still tell the story of a friend of mine who narrowly escaped Dickey's ursine advances through a ruse ("Let me run up and get a nightie, Jim") and left him baying dolefully beneath her dormitory window—"Ciiiindy . . . Ciiiindy"—until the night watchman led him away.

It goes back to the troubadours, this sexual indulgence of poets, this convention that they live by laws of their own. It's inherently offensive, especially when it's exploited by charlatans and bad poets.

Dickey, of course, would have claimed that it was only justified by genius. James Dickey was an unruly, unreliable, impossible man. He was a shambling 220-pound dissertation on the theme "poetic license," a true connoisseur of excess. Yet most of the people he embarrassed, frightened, or compromised managed to forgive him long before he died. Some people couldn't understand Lynn Redgrave's character in the movie *Shine*, when she drops an investment banker to marry pianist David Helfgott, a bizarre schizophrenic. But who with an atom of soul wouldn't at least try to love a man who could play—or write—so well?

Dickey believed, to a dangerous degree, that art justified everything. There was no point in accusing him of calculation. His act was an inseparable part of his art, and like the poems, it wasn't always lovely to behold.

"They don't make men like James Dickey anymore," said novelist Pat Conroy, one of Dickey's eulogists. It's obvious that this is true, not half so obvious *why* it's true. Dickey was a sensual, willful man who had close brushes with death when he was very young, flying combat missions with the 418th Night Fighter Squadron in the Pacific. Defining himself as a survivor, he committed his life to a relentless, sometimes reckless pursuit of unmediated experience.

More often than any other poet, more skillfully than any other, he answered the question, "What does it feel like?" What does it feel like to be a living creature in its skin—in pain, in ecstasy, in terror, in a state of grace? He entered the skins of animals so convincingly, it's a nice conceit to imagine that he's gone, by choice, to "The Heaven of Animals" he created:

> For some of these,
> It could not be the place
> It is, without blood.
> These hunt, as they have done,
> But with claws and teeth grown perfect

As the earthbound understand it, the poetic imagination comes with wings; only Dickey's came equipped with talons, too. In a fallen world where our worst instinct, our herd instinct, is reinforced and manipulated to make consumers and networkers of us all, Dickey followed more ancient instincts. He was a solitary predator— a big cat consumed with curiosity—who made up his own menu as he went along.

It was an impressive menu, unless you were on it. A member of Dickey's family thanked Pat Conroy for glossing over the poet's legendary "appetites." But without the appetites, could we have had the poems? As Dickey himself wrote, in the stunning bravura "For the Last Wolverine"—

> How much the timid poem needs
> The mindless explosion of your rage
> The glutton's internal fire . . .

James Dickey ate more than his share and never apologized. He was no respecter of persons, of marriage vows, of middle-class morals. He was a harsh and brilliant critic whose humility and charity often failed him. No one should be ashamed of failing to like him—only for failing to appreciate what he could do.

A great poet is defined by his antagonists; Dickey collected his enemies as judiciously as he chose his words. Poetry attracts more than its share of Prufrocks, head-dwellers uncomfortable in their skin, city mice petrified of poison ivy and insects. Naturally they detested Dickey, the doubly blessed, who lived so intensely in his skin as well as in his head. Naturally they begrudged him his laurels.

It's fitting that his nemesis was Robert Bly, of *Iron John* fame, who for years has earned a living teaching America's Prufrocks how to reach the Wild Man inside themselves. What a priceless irony, Bly's housebroken males struggling to locate their Wild Men while Dickey received delegations beseeching him to keep his own Wild Man chained in the basement.

Bly called him "a huge blubbery poet," a wide miss on all counts to anyone who read Dickey, or wrestled him. Bly isn't always such a fool. But he was no match for James Dickey, neither on the page nor arm wrestling bard to bard, a showdown Dickey would have given his last caesura to arrange.

Dickey disliked Eliot, dismissed the Beat poets as clowns, and disparaged "the school of Gabby Agony" epitomized by Sylvia Plath and Anne Sexton. To the frustration of his friends and partisans, he backed down from a fight about as readily as his wolverine, and he paid the price.

Between the animus of the poetry establishment, the literary world's generic condescension to Southerners, and the incomprehension of ponderous philistines like Jonathan Yardley of the *Washington Post*, Dickey usually found himself paddling upstream. Fortunately he relished such uncloistered, high-visibility assignments as the space program (he was the first "poet of space"), the Jimmy Carter inauguration, and the Hollywood film of his novel *Deliverance*. They made him a famous man. Yet American poetry did not thrive, or hold its own, in his time. He may be the last poet honored with a six-column obituary in the *New York Times*.

"The world doesn't esteem us very much," he told his last class at the University of South Carolina, "but we are masters of a superior secret."

The handful of poets at the memorial service in Columbia acknowledged the full irony of the last line of "For the Last Wolverine," printed on the program: "Lord, let me die, but not die out."

Poetry is a small world where Dickey's death leaves a huge hole, with no candidates to fill it. But the beauty of a great poet is that he leaves himself a thousand perfect epitaphs, embracing every possibility of death and resurrection. Here are the last lines of his last novel, *To the White Sea*: "I was in it, and part of it. I matched it all. And I will be everywhere in it from now on. You will be able to hear me, just like you're hearing me now. Everywhere in it, for the first time and the last, as soon as I close my eyes."

Yes.

SISTER EVELYN MATTERN

Confession, Dedicated to a Fighting Nun

A FEW YEARS AGO I received a letter of encouragement from Sister Evelyn Mattern, whom I had never met. There was something I'd written that she endorsed; I can't recall the subject. I'd always been an outspoken admirer of the tiny, fearless regiment of Catholic activists, some of the last true friends of the poor and the peace-loving. Sister Evelyn—a tireless, resourceful champion of children, migrant farmworkers, and all voiceless underdogs, was the soul and backbone of that religious community in North Carolina. She offered me kind words and a compliment far too rich to accept: "You must be wonderful," she wrote.

No, it's you who are wonderful, I thought—through the eyes of the rare individual of real excellence, all flawed things look their best. I didn't write back protesting that I was a common struggling sinner, nothing more. But I always hoped to sit down with her someday and talk honestly about how hard it is for most of us to live up to our own moral standards, far less the example set by someone like Evelyn Mattern. This conversation, which I envisioned as a kind of confession, never occurred. When I read that she was dying of lung cancer, I made some notes for an essay I thought I might call "Confession to a Nun, Dying." If it seemed to work, I hoped I'd have the courage to send it (sans title) to her, along with a note expressing my sympathy and my enormous respect for the life she chose to lead.

In October she went home to Philadelphia to die. A few days after she left North Carolina, my stepson died suddenly, at thirty-three. In the midst of our mourning, long before I'd been led to expect, Sister Evelyn died, too, leaving me with my familiar burden of regret and stillborn good intentions.

But the need to confess remains. Disfigured as I am by the sin of pride, I respect only moral authority, bow only to moral superiority as I perceive it. The notion of an earnest Catholic confessing his trivial sins to a pedophile priest makes my skin crawl. So Sister Evelyn is still my choice. I still think it's appropriate, especially so because—as a friend declared to general applause at her farewell celebration—her church had been "foolish" to deny her a priesthood.

Never mind, then, that the other half of this confessional appears to be empty. The disadvantage is that I'll never receive the benefit of her wisdom and good will. The advantage is that I can't embarrass her, as things stand now—the best of us are invariably the most self-effacing. And now I won't make her uncomfortable if I seem to find fault with her church and her God.

I'm no Catholic and have no experience of confessions, except second-hand from my friend Ben Harte, a fallen Irish seminarian on the fast track to hell who used to wear clerical collars and impersonate a priest in the confessionals at St. Patrick's Cathedral. (Ben didn't think people's confessions were funny or pitiful—though I often did, as he related them. He claimed this sacrilege "helped to bridge the distance between God and Ben.")

I never believed that any priest, by virtue of collar or cassock, was one candlewick closer to God than I am. But the symbolic force of confession depends on the conviction that your confessor stands nearer to the Light than you do; no one but an unassuming moral giant like Evelyn Mattern could intercede for a churchless heretic like me. I don't need her to negotiate with a higher power, exactly, but to channel for a higher wisdom—and to intermediate with death.

Forgive me, Sister, for I have sinned. Of the Seven Deadly Sins, only Greed and Envy, cut-rate sins of the underimaginative, have failed to leave deep wounds. Sloth and Gluttony I fight to an honorable draw. Time is taking care of Lust. But Anger and Pride, often indistinguishable, mock my most virtuous resolutions. They cloud my judgment and destroy my peace of mind.

Can any foot soldier learn to love his enemy, or is this a gift reserved for the moral aristocracy? There wasn't a cause Sister Evelyn fought for that I don't endorse. I never failed to deplore injustice, never mislaid the credo that unites religious action and honest journalism—"Comfort the afflicted and afflict the comfortable." But the pursuit of justice—of common decency in public life—sets us in conflict with individuals whose selfishness and cynicism are the shame of our species. Unlike Sister Evelyn, I never failed to hate them vigorously. If these too are God's children, as the virtuous urge me to remember, perhaps God should have had a vasectomy.

And why can't I separate the clean, well-lighted anger of political commitment from the morbid, obsessive anger of personal outrage? I take all injustice personally but abandon all perspective when the victim of injustice is me. Case: A man I know went through a period of stress and mental confusion and decided that I had wronged him, though I had not and told him so. He lived his life in public and circulated this lie as widely as he could. Entreaties and even legal threats failed to muzzle him. Friends assured me that he was a sad case whose paranoia harmed no one but himself. And yet I came to hate him intensely and wish him ill.

After a year of sorrow and misfortune in my family, I resolved that it was time to declare a general amnesty—forgive everyone, even this self-appointed enemy of mine, and start over. I couldn't do it. My anger was a foot taller than my compassion. The list of people I've harmed is a very short one; the list of people I've freely forgiven ("as we forgive those who trespass against us") is shorter yet. My acts of Christian clemency—like my enduring good works—could be listed on a playing card, written out with a magic marker.

Evelyn Mattern, of course, would have protested that she was no saint, that she made her own confessions of human frailty. But she had a saint's patience and a saint's purity of purpose. What set her apart and above? The easy answer is that she had a saint's faith in God, a faith I never achieved. Even as a child I couldn't believe in a god who sees and thinks like human beings, and interferes in our affairs. An all-powerful, hands-on god would have too much to answer for, beginning with terminal cancer for Evelyn Mattern. And ending not with kindergarten bombers or serial killers, but with my excruciating memory of a small, soaked dog staked out shelterless in a cold rain, on someone's front lawn in Yanceyville. Sparrows can fall like hailstones for months, by my observation, without setting off an alarm in heaven.

It's an ancient argument. The faithful deplore our shortsighted-ness, we roll our eyes at their rationalizations. But there's compel-ling evidence—impressed on me most powerfully when I visited the late Philip Berrigan in his jail cell in Edenton—that the per-sonal faith of the Matterns and Berrigans sustains them through trials few agnostics could endure.

Renowned for practical solutions and quantifiable results, Sister Evelyn was also an intellectual, a poet and a self-described mystic.

"The mystic can see God with the eyes of love," she wrote in *Why Not Become Fire?*, her book published in 1999 with artist Helen David Brancato. "Despite the presence of evil in the world, the mystic believes that the universe is ultimately friendly." Subti-tled "Encounters with Women Mystics," the book also argues that mystical experience, which rewards patience and spiritual solitude, is more accessible to women.

From my place here in the confessional, I testify to the truth of

that. To see God with the eyes of love is a miracle, but to view your
fellow man with the eyes of love and the patience of the saints is
a greater one. Perhaps patience is the keystone of all useful compassion, and love without patience—without infinite tolerance—is
impotent. And perhaps testosterone and patience are incompatible.

On the causes dearest to Evelyn Mattern—economic justice,
peace, the environment—I'm proud to be labeled a radical, as she
was sometimes labeled by people inside and outside her church.
The oppressed and afflicted could always count on my voice. But
it's one thing to acknowledge their claim and take their part, quite
another to love them as Mattern did, in all their sweaty, cantanker-
ous, gullible, passive, perverse, ungrateful, and uncomprehending
humanity.

To love not only the helpless and heart-rending, but those
George Bernard Shaw called "the undeserving poor"—that's the
test. To help those who refuse to help themselves, in full knowledge
of all the avoidable ways they harm themselves and each other. It's
hard—hard to see working people without unions or health care,
without security or leverage of any kind in the big-dog economy,
voting prejudice instead of self-interest and marching blindly behind any scoundrel who waves the flag. Item: In Ashe County,
North Carolina, inhabited chiefly by the low-income people who
suffer most in this top-heavy economy and lose their children to
this cynical new war, I found a hand-scrawled poster for a professional wrestling event titled "Flag Fight—American GI vs. Mu-
hammad Ishtar."

It's hard to live with the logical discrepancy between the 5 percent who might conceivably benefit from the policies of Washington's current junta of corporate pirates and parasites, and the 50 percent who vote for them. When thirty-five million Americans live in poverty, when four million families report chronic hunger in a nation of pandemic obesity and obscene luxury, it's hard to forgive comrades who squander their radical sympathies as thought police and verbal vigilantes, providing precious grist for the right-wing spin mills of Rush Limbaugh and Fox News.

It's hard, in short, to love the world as it is instead of the way you think it ought to be. Hard for me. But never hard, if her friends tell it true, for Sister Evelyn. What set her apart, they agree, was her organic, unconditional solidarity with the most miserable and unpromising people, her unaffected enthusiasm for humanity's raw material.

"She sees grand causes through the faces of real people," marveled her old accomplice, the Rev. Collins Kilburn.

How did she manage to love them so? Perhaps only persons touched directly by God can help without judging, serve without scolding, view the slow progress of the human race without wincing. Of course they're very rare—"our own living saint," one friend called Evelyn Mattern—and we only flay ourselves with invidious comparisons. Attracted to mysticism, Mattern must have believed in divine justice. Yet she fought as if she believed, with me, that the justice we fight for is the only justice we receive.

But this was a confession, not a eulogy. I plead most guilty to the sin of Exasperation, Anger's querulous, high-pitched little brother, a rose-colored rather than a cardinal sin. In Dante's ten-tiered hell, he must have reserved a chilly balcony somewhere for the exasperated. If it's primarily a failure of patience, and gender is a mitigating circumstance, I'll enter any plea that reduces my penance.

But there's another matter, another sin. They say Evelyn Mattern "radiated a contagious joy and a definite, deep-settled peace"—a joy, a peace beyond the reach of those who do not find the universe friendly. In a poem my brother sent me once, Jorge Luis Borges speaks of "this shadow of having been a brooding man." The poem is called "Remorse" and it begins "I have committed the worst sin of all that a man can commit. I have not been happy."

How many Hail Marys for that one?

JAMES STILL

A Man of the World

The earth shall rise up where he lies
With steady reach, and permanent.
A shroud of cedars be his mound
This shield of hills his monument.

James Still (1906–2001), "Shield of Hills"

N A COUNTRY tribute to James Still's longevity, one of his neighbors told him "You're the last possum up the tree." The last of his generation in Knott County, Kentucky, the neighbor meant to say. But Still, who died in April a few weeks short of his ninety-fifth birthday, was also the last of the undisputed "Greatest Generation" of American writers. William Faulkner, Ernest Hemingway, Robert Penn Warren, Thomas Wolfe, F. Scott Fitzgerald, Thornton Wilder, John Dos Passos, Allen Tate, and John Steinbeck were all born within a single decade at the turn of the last century, and it was their fiction and poetry that introduced most of the world's readers to the riches of American literature.

James Still, born in 1906, was the youngest of these giants and the least celebrated. There are respectable readers, even English teachers, who fail to recognize his name. In contrast with ceremonies for the great Eudora Welty, mourned like an empress last summer by Mississippi and the literate world, Still's wake was an Appalachian family affair. His limited renown, his admirers argue, was due entirely to regional prejudice and Still's reluctance to practice our culture-defining art of self-promotion.

"I think that up there in Knott County, well off the main track of the literary world, Still became a nearly perfect writer," wrote Wendell Berry. "His stories consist of one flawless sentence after another."

Such reckless praise invites a close reading of the venerable Sage of Hindman. Take the time. Though Still outlived all the rest, he was not prolific; his pursuit was perfection, not saturation. If you read the classic Appalachian novel *River of Earth* (Viking, 1940), the new collected poems (*From the Mountain, From the Valley*, University of Kentucky Press, 2001), and the 1977 story collection *Pattern of a Man* from Gnomon Press, you haven't covered James Still by a long shot but you've measured him fairly. If you're not impressed—if you're new to Still and you're not astonished—then possibly literature isn't your strong suit after all.

Acclaim has not been stingy. Poet Delmore Schwartz, hardly an Appalachian partisan, once called *River of Earth* "a symphony," and wrote of Still, "This man has something special." For his humanity and the psychological subtlety of his fiction, Still was described as an Appalachian Chekhov; for his populist humor with its marbling of black irony, he was compared with Mark Twain; in his fierce hermit's independence and minute observation of the natural world, he reminded readers of Henry David Thoreau. Stories like "Mrs. Razor," "Maybird Upshaw," and "A Master Time" are tone-perfect, simultaneously heart-vexing and hysterical, and so finely crafted that Wendell Berry rightly describes one as "almost a miracle." They'd have dazzled Mark Twain or even the author of *Dubliners*.

Still's loyalty to the native dialect of Eastern Kentucky made him a hero in Appalachia but may have cost him the international reputation he deserved. His characters speak as their models spoke, in the vernacular of his neighbors on Troublesome Creek before the Second World War. To jaded urban ears a story in any regional dialect sounds like folklore, and critics and publishers are among the most jaded of urban animals. ("Thus an incoherent culture condescends to a coherent one," as Wendell Berry laments.)

Still himself was too quick to concede the point, once calling his stories "a social diagram of a folk society such as hardly exists today." But *Moby-Dick* is no less powerful because summer celebrities have replaced Nantucket whalers. *War and Peace* loses nothing human because Pierre's lost society of aristocrats lies buried under centuries of social upheaval and disaster. No "true" story, crafted by a writer of genius, ever becomes archaic.

James Still, a subsistence homesteader in a time before paved roads, a man who favored overalls and straw hats, claimed the label "hillbilly" never bothered him: "I count it as an honor, except when used as a slur." But before he settled in Knott County he earned three university degrees, including a master's in English from Vanderbilt, where he was a contemporary of the famous Fugitive poets. Among his countless prizes and distinctions were two Guggenheim Fellowships; as a younger man he summered at the Yaddo and MacDowell writer's colonies with most of the literary lions of his day. By standards far more cosmopolitan than Knott County's, he was a man of the world—a traveler who visited twenty-six countries and made fourteen trips to Central America to study Mayan culture.

Yet for most of seventy years you could find him in Hindman. When an artist of Still's stature lives so long in a place so remote he begins to draw pilgrims and generate myths, some of a quasi-saintly nature, like the story of the suit coat he left hanging on a bush for months because he refused to disturb a bird who'd built a nest in its sleeve.

Still loved the birds and beasts. But he was no St. Francis, no beaming haloed presence. He was proud, private, sometimes a little prickly. He could be flattered, but he wasn't one to roll over and wag his tail every time someone gushed, "I love your work." He could be distant, even impatient with academics, poetasters, and literary day-trippers. He preferred the company of children, animals, and poets—creatures without agendas, without *careers*.

"I've often remarked that he would be happy if there were only children in the world," said his friend Mike Mullins, director of the Hindman Settlement School where Still had served as *genius loci* since 1932.

"He's very innocent in a certain way," wrote my wife, Lee Smith, a writer with whom Still loved to flirt. "I don't mean to say he's childish. But there's a freshness and originality of language that I think is childlike. He has access to that part of himself that most of us have lost."

Not surprisingly, the narrator of *River of Earth* is a seven-year-old boy. At Still's funeral, one speaker revealed that "my dog Jack," immortalized in the poem "Those I Want in Heaven With Me, Should There Be Such a Place," was a dog the poet's father had given away when Still was seven years old—a wound he nursed for most of a century.

In his seventies Still began to write for children, retelling—inimitably—Mother Goose rhymes and the "Jack" tales of Appalachian storytellers. When someone asked him why the dean of Appalachian literature was fooling with nursery rhymes, he replied, "I've been foolish the whole time." At the same time he was consuming literary magazines and journals; if you doubted that he kept abreast of the latest trends in fiction and poetry, he was always poised to set you straight.

Hillbilly intellectual, log-cabin hermit with a thousand luggage stickers, the oldest possum with the youngest heart—James Still sounds like a walking circus of contradictions. But contradictions trouble people who live and think inside the box; if Still ever knew the box existed, he never let on.

Conventional souls, often envious, call a man like James Still "a character." He wasn't an eccentric so much as a natural man who found a sanctuary where his idiosyncrasies were indulged. In Kentucky his world was subdivided by creeks and ridges, and among them he found all that he ever needed to write about. Despite his travels there seems to be only one published piece—a poem set in Belize on one of Still's Mayan expeditions—that didn't find its inspiration in Knott County.

At his memorial service one speaker after another tried to express how entertaining it was to know Mr. Still. (You called him "Mr." Still unless you were a writer he admired, a woman he fancied, or his rare equal in years—a "Brother to Methuselum" like ancient Uncle Mize in one of his best stories.) They labored to capture his grand sense of mischief—his dark, deep-set eyes fairly glittered with it, right up to the end. They remembered him stretched out snoring on the reading table in the library, and his delight in smuggling six-packs and Kentucky Fried Chicken to the Trappist monks at Gethsemani Abbey, which housed that other garrulous hermit Thomas Merton.

It started me thinking about longevity. It's obvious that there are no special extensions for the pious or the virtuous, or the rich or wise either. Yet here was the oldest man for miles around, and by far the most interesting. Maybe Fate or the Reaper or whoever cuts our strings is actually a connoisseur like Scheherazade's Sultan, and couldn't bear to interrupt Mr. Still in the middle of a wonderful story.

The most eloquent eulogist was Appalachian scholar Loyal Jones. To honor Still, Jones said, is to honor "art and integrity, and the need for some people to be different from the rest of us."

For me it was an august honor to do a couple of readings with him; I saved the programs. I excused his attentions to my wife because he was almost forty years older than we were, though no doubt I underestimated him.

He was a strange and unforgettable man, and most people who knew him must have moments when he seems present, yet. One morning I was reading Still's collected poems on a mountainside in North Carolina—a deliberate exercise, with one eye on the blue ridges and one hand on my dog. I was deep in "Year of the Pigeons" when an emerald hummingbird descended on a flame-red phlox plant just six feet away. The poem and the bird struggled for my attention until I imagined a voice I knew as well as the ageless face that I often studied on the sly. "Set that poem aside," it said, "and mind the hummingbird."

MARSHALL FRADY

Son of a Preacher Man

The Southerner always tended to believe with
his blood rather than his intellect.
—Marshall Frady, *Southerners*

I NEVER MET MARSHALL Frady, though we knew so many of
the same people it seems uncanny that I missed him. We even
survived the same apprenticeship as writers, among the hopeful
anonymous at Time-Life and Post-Newsweek. I can imagine what
he went through at those places. My own prose style, naturally
expansive, still turns timid at times from the savage abuse it suffered at the hands of newsmagazine editors, some of them—luck

of the draw—not sagacious old pros but tone-deaf philistines and phrase-butchers. Frady alone betrayed no scars. He managed to nurse his polysyllabic style through the lean years and see it bloom extravagantly under kinder editors, most notably Willie Morris at Harper's.

It was a prose too exuberant to die. An ironic consequence of Frady's untimely death at sixty-four is that his books (seven, including a Penguin biography of Martin Luther King, Jr.) began to receive more of the attention they always deserved. Readers rediscovered a mode of English expression like no other, North or South. Or rather, like one other. A steadfast son of the South— a Baptist preacher's boy from Georgia—Frady never forswore his debt to William Faulkner, to Faulkner's native themes and obsessions and also to his headlong, tempest-tossed, punctuation-defying prose. He even spoke in what his friends called "Faulknerian patois."

"Faulkner is an experience that a lot of Southern boys spend the rest of their lives trying to recover from," Frady wrote in his introduction to *Southerners*. He didn't try as hard as some. In New York they called his work New Journalism—because it was nothing like the old journalism, I suppose. Nobody bothered to compare it with *The Sound and the Fury*. I've seen word counts on some of Faulkner's sentences; I'm not young enough to take a week and count them on my own. But on page 282 of *Southerners*, in an essay titled "The South Domesticated," there's a 255-word sentence without one semicolon (and just three dashes). I won't even claim it's one of his longest.

Actually it's a damn fine sentence, too. You have to take care, when you write about Frady, not to write *like* Frady, or attempt it. As a stylist, he may have been one of the great subversive influences of his generation. Echoes of his hard-riding, whip-at-the-ready prose performances turned up in everything from free verse to postmodern fiction. But few novelists—and no one writing biography and literary journalism, as he did—ever equalled Frady's love for the sound of loaded clauses breaking like storm waves against the fragile sandbars of the reader's resistance.

There's every indication that he was born with that style, and employed stream-of-consciousness to write home to his parents from Bible camp.

"He had it from the start, absolutely," recalls Joe Cumming, who hired Frady for *Newsweek*'s Atlanta bureau in 1966. "I asked him to write a quick bio sketch, you know, just so we'd have a writing sample in his file. He sat down and wrote seventeen pages that sounded like Shakespeare to me. It was a talent wasted at the bureau, of course—we knew he'd be moving on. But I used to defend his style against people who thought it was too exotic."

Apparently Frady aspired to live a life that matched his prose. At sixteen he ran off to Cuba to join the revolution—three times—and reached Havana once, but never managed to hook up with Fidel Castro or Che Guevara. ("I never made it to the poetry going on in those mythic mountains.") Castro became a lifelong obsession. In 1973 Frady ran up a two-month, $17,000 expense account in Mexico City, pleading unsuccessfully with the Cuban embassy for a *Playboy* interview with Fidel. The two met at last in 1993. Frady was working on a biography of Castro when he died.

Marc Cooper of the *Nation*, who accompanied Frady on the

Mexican expedition, describes the demonic disciplines of a picturesque writer in his prime: "He went to the pharmacy next door and bought a roll of amphetamine tablets. Then he bought a fifth of J&B and, at sunset, locked himself in his hotel room. The next morning I was stunned to see that he'd been up all night. The wrappers for the speed were empty. As was the bottle of scotch. Crumpled paper littered the room. 'Look, I've got it, I've got it,' he said, and handed me a single piece of paper."

"If anyone could be described as a hopeless romantic," says Joe Cumming, "it was Marshall."

Frady missed the revolution in Cuba but found one waiting for him back home. The civil rights movement was the crucible for a generation of Southern journalists who remain among the bright lights of a rapidly dimming profession—to name a few would be to slight too many. Some of them took greater risks and delivered more battlefront dispatches, but no one articulated the experience more eloquently than Frady.

"By lucky accident," he wrote in *Southerners*, "I happened to be writing about the South at one of those climactic moments of truth when everything—past and present, inward and outward—suddenly glares into a resolution larger and more urgent than its ordinary aspect."

In an interview thirty years later, he evoked "the mighty moral drama of the movement in the '60s, which for a lot of journalists who covered it was like a kind of existential Damascus Road experience, a season of super-reality when good and evil somehow hit the bottom of the lungs in a way they never have quite since."

It's hard to ignore the suggestion that everything since Selma, since Memphis, had been anticlimax. I'm aware of the risks taken when you biographize the biographer, when you journalize the journalist. Marshall Frady anticipated his own psychobiographers. You can profile Frady just by quoting Frady; he never held much back. "Still secretly and irredeemably a kind of shabby romantic, still incorrigibly given to posturing," he says of himself at thirty. "He had begun to be haunted that his epitaph might well be: 'His was a life of brave beginnings . . .' "

I suspect Frady was angling for a better epitaph when he secured Jesse Jackson to preach his funeral. ("He could paint pictures with words," offered Jackson. "Even in his normal conversation he was a painter.") His long relationship with Jackson, who was famously fond of him and impatient with him, grew out of the Movement that provided them both with a season of epiphany and moral certainty, a "super-reality" after which many an encore seemed forced or false. Like Jackson, Frady was a gifted, ambitious individual who felt himself chosen for a higher calling that was not always recognized or encouraged. His biography of Jackson, *Jesse*, was a shrewd reassessment that went a long way toward rehabilitating a familiar figure who had been reduced—most unjustly, Frady argued—almost to a figure of fun.

Jesse balanced Jackson's outsized ego—"Not only does Jesse believe in God, Jesse believes God believes in him," one of Jackson's friends told Frady—against "a creative largeness of moral vision" and a "galvanic" capacity for personal connection he shared with only two public figures in Frady's experience: George Wallace and ("in his later days") Bobby Kennedy.

"Forever an unfinished hero," Frady called Jackson. But the

most convincing depiction of heroism Frady ever wrote is his eyewitness account of Jesse's Gulf War mission to Baghdad in 1990—Jackson facing down Saddam Hussein and his secret police to extract hostages, life by life, with an unrehearsed display of compassion and resolve, cutting the kind of figure John Wayne could only fake for cameras. Hundreds were rescued. Iraqis were awed. But the State Department dismissed Jackson's feat with a curt "Thanks, pal" and the media, as usual, portrayed him as a showboating meddler.

That's the story of Jackson's life, as Frady told it: an ultimately tragic figure whose worst moments were magnified while his best were discounted. And Frady reminds us that all black leaders, even Reverend King, have had to clear a much higher bar to win respect. He loved Jackson, and identified with him, for the reach that exceeded his grasp—as the man who would be King, even Gandhi, in a country that wanted him to be Eddie Murphy.

But it was Jackson's personal magnetism that fascinated Frady, his rare ability to project and connect and make the faithful weep and shout. Ever since his father loomed above him with the holy scriptures on his tongue, the charisma of the "mass communicators, mass communers" had been Frady's special area of study. His major books comprise a gallery of charismatics. Only preachers and politicians, only those who risk everything on audience response need apply (and no Yankees). Jackson, Wallace, and Billy Graham had nothing in common except their unnatural grip on ordinary people—and their desperate need to exercise it.

As Frady saw him, Graham was a man of natural decency and sincerity, and very limited intelligence, whose simple faith and odor of sanctity were exploited by cynical presidents. Graham was "the indestructible American innocent," a country boy bewildered by his own celebrity—Frady compares him to Candide and to Melville's Billy Budd—and his great spiritual crisis was not a loss of faith in God but a loss of faith, after Watergate, in Richard Nixon. Another cleric described him to Frady as "God's own divine bumpkin."

George Wallace, "the greatest of the American demagogues, the classic of his species" was revealed to Frady as "curiously vague and weightless" in his private life, an empty suit, a political windup doll that only seemed alive when it was working crowds and pressing flesh. Like Graham, Wallace could never stand to be alone, and Frady found in him, as well, "a childlike naivete." "The stumpy, dingy, surly orphan of American politics," Frady called him, but he pitied Wallace, too, especially after the bullet in his spine ended the hands-on, "glandular" politicking that was all Wallace lived for.

Unlike most reporters, Frady wasn't probing for the flaws, for the feet of clay in his subjects' brogans; he took those for granted. What obsessed him was the populist mystery of their connection to crowds, and the high stakes they played for: power and high office, justice—souls.

Righteousness was his compass. Back through the Movement and the martyrdom of King, the dark feral passages of the race wars, back even to his infatuation with Castro and his stunned teenager's response to *For Whom the Bell Tolls*, Frady meant to stand on the side of the angels. In these "communicators" whose art transfixed him, he was always looking for a trace of the hero, for the divine spark. In the ones the people followed, how much angel could he find?

This hunger for virtue is a Baptist, a Jesus thing, Frady tells us. And I thought, no, it's a small-town, middle-class thing—all of us brought up in quiet places by upright, thoughtful, honorable people start out on the side of the angels, wander offside, and spend the rest of our lives trying to find it again. But I realized Frady's case was more acute when Billy Graham asked him, "What is your own spiritual standing?" I would have stammered and stared. But Frady answered promptly: "Well, I don't know that I have accepted Jesus exactly in the sense you would mean, but I believe in him, I love him, he's a living reality to me."

The last portrait in *Southerners* is of Will Campbell, the writer and outlaw Baptist minister Frady taxonomizes as "a funda-mentalist gospel existentialist," and who was described to me as Frady's "father confessor." It happens that Rev. Campbell, who defies classification, was the man I'd have chosen for my own confessor if I'd had enough holiness left in me to make regular pilgrimages to Mt. Juliet, Tennessee. But I did make one when Marshall Frady died.

"Frady is a hard man to describe," Campbell told me. "It was a different language he spoke, no matter what the subject. Who else used words like 'soliloquize' at breakfast? 'Let us retreat to the salt mines,' he'd say when he went to work. But there was an authentic person behind all those words; if he promised you something, you could put it in the bank.

"He was a big talker, a big liver, too, you know, but in a way he never left his father's fireside. He had that old Baptist commitment he was always affirming. Haunted by his faith. We won't meet another one like him."

Like all pure originals, Frady had his detractors. One prominent liberal journalist complained that "he was in love with the sound of his own words"—guilty as charged, I suspect—and that his supercharged syntax too often "lost it on the curves." The charges against him seem to boil down to a single judgment: whether the gorgeous language overwhelms the message or obscures the personalities.

If my vote counted, I'd say, "Not often." Whose book would you read, the writer who notes Congressman Mendel Rivers's "soft Southern drawl" —and couldn't in all likelihood tell a Charleston drawl from the Richmond version—or the one who describes "a mossy purr . . . an ambient and wraith-breathed delivery, as elusive and stealthy as fog rippling slowly over a swamp of hyacinths and water moccasins"? It's your call.

"The 'how' becomes the 'what' when you read Marshall," says his friend Franklin Ashley. "The way it's put together is inseparable from the story itself. No one else approached that fusion."

There's a prophetic element, too—not biblical but wry and Menckenesque. It was Frady, twenty-five years ago, who predicted that the adjective "Christian" would one day describe everything from theme parks to nightclubs to rock 'n' roll. His eyeball-to-eyeball with Saddam Hussein is worth reading, too. But Frady's gallery of saints and sinners, beginning with *Southerners*, is a visionary achievement like nothing else in the literature. To my ear, it's a Song of the South sung with near-perfect pitch, neither sweet nor sour, seasoned righteously with salt and soul.

If an individual from Wisconsin claims the Badger State had one just like Earl Long or Mendel Rivers—or George Wallace or Martin Luther King, Jr. —my response is to say, "The hell it did, buddy," and refer him to the collected works of Marshall Frady. They should be required reading as long as the South makes a point of being the South—a point perhaps finite in time—and afterward for anyone who wants to know what it was like to live in "this peculiar dream-province of the Republic," as he called it, during the tumultuous half-century when Frady stood his never-wordless watch.

KIRK VARNEDOE

A Prophet from Savannah

Though modern art has often dreamed of a closed society,
it can function only in an open one.
—Kirk Varnedoe, "A Fine Disregard"

I N COLLEGE, MOST of us are too self-conscious and too anxious
about our own uncertain fortunes to make accurate judgments
of our peers. We're attracted to style without substance, often to
individuals with neither if a deadly jump shot or a famous family
is part of the package they present.

The hardest thing of all, when you're a boy—it was a single-
sex New England college I attended—is to predict which of your

contemporaries will become men who make genuine, lasting contributions to something greater than the alumni fund. Of the men I knew at Williams College, only two have been asked to come back and deliver the commencement address. One was a blowhard opportunist who achieved high office in Washington by endearing himself to right-wing politicians, and financial success as the author of lowbrow bestsellers urging Americans to tone up their morals. Eventually he squandered most of his money and all of his political capital as a compulsive high-rolling gambler, the kind of mega-sucker casinos milk solicitously in private rooms.

The other commencement speaker was a much more interesting case. One Friday night in the fall of my junior year I found myself—uncharacteristically—at a football pep rally with a towering bonfire and large posters foretelling the mayhem the home eleven would soon inflict on Amherst. I noticed that the artwork on these posters was a great improvement over last year's and asked if anyone knew who the artist might have been. "Sophomore named Varnedoe," someone replied. "He's a football player—lineman. A Southerner."

That was the first time I heard the name. On the Sunday after the last football game, while boys with thick necks and buzz cuts, liberated from training, stalked the campus in various stages of alcohol poisoning, I was in bed at noon trying to sleep through a certain hangover. There was a rough knock on the door and two imposing figures hovered over my bed: the larger one was an ex-Marine noncom named Westy Saltonstall and the other—I rubbed my eyes and reached for my bifocals—appeared to be wearing an entire suit, jacket and pants, of cotton printed with Budweiser labels.

"Crowther," croaked Saltonstall, "get dressed, you maggot, we're going to Cozy's. You know Kirk Varnedoe?"

Saltonstall, four beers into his Parris Island persona, was not a force I ever chose to resist. If not the biggest, he was surely the oldest man on campus, and his family had held half the first-class tickets on the Mayflower, or so we provincials believed. I pulled on my jeans while the kid in the Bud suit grinned at me. Did Kirk Varnedoe make a vivid first impression? Well, his suit did. Drinking was ritualized at Williams, to a degree that makes me cringe today. Drinking uniforms and accessories were not uncommon. One clown in KA wore a horned Viking helmet, like Hägar the Horrible in the comics; I myself owned a hard hat with my name stenciled on it, from a summer job in the steel mills. Even so, the Bud suit was a statement. I guess Kirk was saying, "I'm from Savannah, where people party seriously, whether you Yankees know it or not."

Those who dressed to drink often overplayed their roles, in my opinion, but this sophomore had a nice, recognizably Southern reserve about him. After all these years I thought I might have imagined the suit—a drinker's hallucination. But among Kirk's many obituaries I found the same suit mentioned by Marcia Vetrocq, who knew him in graduate school at Stanford. I wonder who's wearing it now. It was a limited secret that Varnedoe, by Williams standards, was a drinker of no epic capacity who sometimes suffered grievously for weekend excesses. Another secret I can guess at, because it was my secret, too. The part of Williams we inhabited held hard work and serious study in serious contempt, so our academic enthusiasms and best grades remained carefully concealed from many of our friends.

Varnedoe must have been taking in something besides liquid calories at Williams because six years later he had a PhD in art history and was already an acknowledged expert on Rodin. He taught at Columbia and NYU and at thirty-eight won a MacArthur "genius" grant, an honor that at least symbolically left the rest of us far behind. At forty-two, a professor with no museum experience, he was named curator of painting and sculpture at the Museum of Modern Art. It was, and is, the most influential job in the fluid, insular, fiercely contentious world of modern art. Just two decades past his last Amherst game, the lineman from Savannah was sitting in the chair where the most critical decisions in his profession are made—"the conscientious, continuous, resolute distinction of quality from mediocrity," according to his Olympian predecessor Alfred Barr. The Modern and its chief curator serve the American art establishment as a kind of aesthetic Supreme Court, and most of their rulings are beyond appeal.

This seat of power was the culmination of a spectacular rise, and Varnedoe gave every appearance of having been born for the job. With his rough-sketched Barrymore profile, his Low Country manners, and the Italian suits that somewhere replaced his Bud jacket—and his stylish, talented wife, the sculptor Elyn Zimmerman—he added a glamour that was brand new to the museum trade, and catnip to the celebrity-hungry tabloids that patrol Manhattan society.

Outside New York and the cloistered art world, the name Varnedoe might not be a household word. None of his eighteen books can be purchased in airports. But among artists and art professionals, his was a presence you could only compare to Tiger Woods or Russell Crowe. When he delivered the Mellon Lectures at the National Gallery in 2003, not long before he died, the museum was forced to rig extra auditoriums with audio relays. The lines wouldn't have been longer if Picasso had come back from the dead to sign autographs. Our Georgia boy was the closest thing to a rock star that art history has ever produced.

Marcia Vetrocq, his friend at Stanford, remembered him in just such an aura—"a motorcycle-riding rock star, impossibly handsome in a sea of sun-deprived academics."

"Unfortunately for us in the art world," Edward Goldman eulogized on NPR, "there is no heir apparent to his unique brand of magic."

We were all proud of Varnedoe, but of course we were amazed. Neither the talent nor the glamour had been readily apparent at school. His trademark rendition of the scabrous fifty-eight-verse rugby ballad "Eskimo Nell" provoked a near-incident on a flight to London, according to his teammates on the Williams College Rugby Club. They offered a consensus: "Anyone who knew Kirk in the '60s would find it hard to believe that he is now so well respected."

What do we remember? Obviously he was thoughtful, cut from different cloth than the guy with the Viking helmet. He'd give you this loopy grin, but if you paid attention you could see that something else was happening with his eyes. Alert, he was. Curious, aware. But an alpha intellectual and A-list celebrity, a sex symbol

for the girls of Mensa? Come on. As his brother Sam said about the
young Kirk in his eulogy, "The kid was bright, fun, and engaging,
but he wasn't remarkable."

Some inevitable connection between the boy and the man has
always been a leap of faith for biographers, a bridge of suggestion
where insight and scholarship fail. Modern celebrity is much complicated by the media and the combustible cult of celebrity itself.
"The spotlight hit the boy," Simon and Garfunkel sing—in another context—"he flew away." Varnedoe was puzzled by his own
image. You don't study art history to become rich and famous; it
isn't like buying a guitar and a spangled body suit and driving to
Nashville. Kirk had a comical response when the New York City
gossip kittens labeled him "a hunk" and "a dreamboat." He looked
in the mirror.

"If the definition of beauty is symmetry, this ain't it," he told
his old Savannah friend Albert Scardino. "My face is skewed to
the right because my jaw juts out one way and my forehead is out
of balance and my ears don't match and I have all these moles all
over the place."

The whole was more photogenic than the sum of its parts. But
aside from the occasional photograph at a black-tie function, surrounded by famous faces, the man we knew at Williams seemed
essentially unchanged. (Though his hair, by my rural standards,
got a little too spiky for awhile in the '90s.) He was loyal to a fault.
When he delivered the commencement address at Williams, he
might have quoted Alfred Barr, Clement Greenberg, or some such
oracle of modern art. Instead he quoted me, from a reactionary
pro-drinking essay, "The Night People," that I'd published in the

Williams *Record* as my parting shot. When Varnedoe organized his first major exhibition at the Modern, the controversial "High and Low: Modern Art and Popular Culture," many art critics were brutally dismissive—but none of them noted that he'd commissioned the show's video guide from an old rugby buddy who was down on his luck.

He kept up with people, and if the old crowd never seemed to resent his conspicuous success—as they sometimes resented classmates who became corporate overlords—it was partly because he cut a prominent figure in a field they scarcely understood. For most of us, the Great Varnedoe was just an excellent adventure we could share vicariously.

This tendency to exempt him from envy was not shared by the art community, never known for its easygoing magnanimity. Kirk was a flashy, well-connected outsider who never earned his stripes in the curatorial boot camps, and the intramural sniping commenced even before he was installed at the Modern. One bone of fierce contention was an ad for Barney's men's store, photographed by Annie Leibovitz, with a mugging Varnedoe looking suave and surly in a suit by Ermenegildo Zegna. A neglected footnote was that his modeling fee went to New York's Coalition for the Homeless.

By the time "High and Low" went up, in 1990, the wolves were circling and salivating.

"A textbook case for the maxim that an exhibition top-heavy in masterpieces can still be a disaster," sniffed Roberta Smith of the *New York Times*, a special enemy of the curator she chose to see, at the time, as a presumptuous South Georgia playboy. Varnedoe's retrospectives for the Southern-born painters Cy Twombly (1994) and Jasper Johns (1996) were more successful with the highbrow critics. But the ad hominem backbiting never truly abated until the announcement in 1996 that he was being treated for advanced colon cancer.

That's New York for you. According to Robert Storr, his colleague at the Modern, Varnedoe was "clearly wounded by the intemperate nature of some of the attacks." If so, they weren't wounds he licked in public. We'd been out of touch after I left New York—though he kept sending me invitations to openings—but I began to see Kirk more often in the '90s. The meanness he had provoked was a mystery to me, just as it was a mystery why all other museum curators were invisible scholars and Kirk was like Sky Masterson in *Guys and Dolls*. It was in 1998, when he had apparently recovered from his cancer, that I finally began to understand what the boy in the Bud suit had made of himself, and why I should pay attention.

He had just opened his Jackson Pollock retrospective to wide acclaim. He invited a few of his Williams friends to tour the exhibition at eight in the morning, before the museum opened, and educated us painting by painting as we walked through it with our wives. In all honesty, I'd never been a Pollock enthusiast. English majors, with their weakness for narrative structure, are resistant to abstract expressionism, and Pollock's neurotic chaos is especially intimidating.

After an hour of looking at Pollock's paintings through Varnedoe's eyes, I saw Pollock as I'd never seen him before. More dramatically, I saw Kirk Varnedoe as I'd never seen him before. Varnedoe at fifty was a spellbinder, as they used to call them, who could have sold Pollock to a Pre-Raphaelite or Andy Warhol soup cans to Cosimo de Medici.

It's hard to admit that someone you knew as a teenager is a genius of any kind. Yet here was a pure genius of the lectern at the top of his form. It was a rare privilege to watch him work with the paintings themselves. At the Mellon Lectures I learned that he was just as good with a carousel of slides—a magician, like Ricky Jay with a deck of playing cards. He could dazzle and hypnotize. When I asked him for the text of his Mellon lectures, he explained—with mixed pride and sheepishness—that he never lectured from a text, or even from notes. The same memory that conquered the formidable "Eskimo Nell" had somehow absorbed the entire chronicle and spectacle of modern art.

"Preacherly" was a word someone used to describe him at the podium. "Art is my religion," he told TV's Charlie Rose. And I recalled the classroom style of Lane Faison, Kirk's mentor, the legendary Williams art professor whose students now run about half of America's major museums. Faison, also a maestro of the slide projector, approached the study of art as if it were some vigorous outdoor sport, some voyage of discovery for hardy bronzed sailors, not "sun-deprived academics."

"For Lane, art was very much a personal experience," Varnedoe said once. "It was between you and the object."

Varnedoe was Faison's perfect disciple. "For Kirk, art was as physical and pleasurable as being knocked down by a wave," said his former student, *New Yorker* critic Adam Gopnik. Artist Chuck Close praised "his passion for objects over ideas." From his ideal perch at the Modern, Varnedoe became prophet, high priest, and principle evangelist for his own cult of strenuous engagement, his church for aestho-athletes driven to probe and pierce and wrestle with works of art until they yielded their secrets. If art can spawn fauvism, Dadaism, and the Ashcan School, why hesitate to coin a name for Varnedoe's faith? "Sinewism" seems to work. My coinage may not catch on with the art historians, but brief research reveals that Kirk loved the word *sinew* and used it: in Giacometti's sculptures he found "the resilient sinews of humanity."

Genius and hard work notwithstanding—friends say he worked eighteen-hour days—it was a miracle of good fortune for Varnedoe to win the one job on the planet where his gifts and passions could make the biggest difference. Such favors are rarely granted by the gods, and the gods never fail to exact a price. Varnedoe spent fourteen years at the Modern, nearly half of them in the shadow of a life-threatening illness. The cancer recurred in 2001 and eventually metastasized. As treatments began to fail him, Kirk put the last of his strength into his Mellon Lectures—a six-part, nine-hour defense of abstract art, titled "Pictures of Nothing," which became one of those triumphs of will and spirit that eyewitnesses make into stories to tell their children. His final lecture was an eloquent, prophetic flight of free association. None of us who were there, not even those few who raised a glass with him afterwards, could point to any sign that this was not a man at the peak of his powers. Less than three months later he was dead, at fifty-seven.

"To the last, Kirk considered himself to be a lucky man," wrote Marcia Vetrocq, echoing the last public words of a New York idol of another era, the great Lou Gehrig, dying of ALS: "I consider myself the luckiest man on the face of the earth."

Gehrig was another big, good-looking jock who in his life was dealt many good hands and one very bad one. Varnedoe chose to introduce his final lecture with the less-quoted last words of the android Roy Batty (Rutger Hauer) in Ridley Scott's film *Blade Runner*: "I've seen things you people wouldn't believe—attack ships on fire off the shoulder of Orion, bright as magnesium; I rode on the back decks of a blinker and watched C-beams glitter in the dark near the Tannhauser Gate. All those moments will be lost in time, like tears in rain. Time to die."

A certain percentage of the overflow audience understood that Varnedoe was dying, and at these words, of course, that percentage was in tears.

"There it is," Kirk concluded when his last slide faded from the screen. "I have shown it to you. It has been done. It is being done. And because it can be done, it will be done. And now I am done."

I never saw him again, after that astonishing Sunday at the National Gallery. The apostle of Sinewism had issued his last encyclical. But once you've heard a great preacher, you're bound to sample his version of the gospel. Varnedoe's books and essays have been as much of a revelation to me as his virtuosity in the pulpit. We assign the highest intelligence to those who agree with us, and without ever discussing anything philosophical—sports and friends, and maybe France, made up the whole of our conversations—this brilliant Varnedoe and I had arrived at many of the same conclusions.

He used his influence to oppose the dreary, reductive Marxism and Marx-inflected theory that casts us all, even artists, as helpless prisoners of our own narrow context. Everything an artist creates is predictable, according to these grim antihumanist heretics, if we can fix him within the correct contextual coordinates. To these theorists art is an incidental by-product of the class struggle, and genius, inspiration, even talent and quality are decadent, repressive elitist notions.

Anyone who ever loved art or literature believes intuitively that this is philistine rubbish, that it's always what *can't* be predicted, what's individual and eccentric—the sudden insight, the rogue notion—that lights up the canvas, the page, and the world. Against reductive theory, Varnedoe declared his belief in "the individual human consciousness, for all its flaws and deforming optics, as our prime resource and treasure." The title of his most definitive book on modern art, *A Fine Disregard*, comes from the story that rugby was invented when an English soccer player, displaying what his commemorative plaque calls "a fine disregard for the rules," suddenly picked up the ball and ran with it.

Varnedoe scorned inevitability and worshiped the random. As a literary critic, I always declared the same faith and fought the same fight, against the same ferocious philistines. Somehow we belonged to the same church, Varnedoe and I. Was there any significance in the fact, confirmed after Kirk's death by his brother Sam, that we both carried not-so-secret torches for Emmylou Harris? (He also loved Elvis and Sam Cooke.) The novelist Kurt Vonnegut, with whom Kirk was occasionally confused, invented the concept of the karass, a group of people with something important but subtle in common. Opposed to the karass was the granfalloon, a group with something utterly superficial in common—like Williams College alumni.

Often as not, what intrigued Varnedoe intrigues me. Especially the book he never wrote but mentioned in every interview—his book on "how Rauschenberg, Johns, and Twombly, three Southern boys, changed the world." In the near-century since H. L. Mencken dismissed the South as "the Sahara of the Bozart," Southern artists have struggled to be taken seriously by the New York mandarins, or even by their own regional museums. It was no coincidence that Varnedoe, a Southerner unexpectedly appointed chief mandarin, devoted two of his major retrospectives to Johns and Twombly. As loyal to his roots as to his friends, he had big plans for the South's undernourished reputation, but he ran out of time.

Since the '50s, modern art has revered Johns, from South Carolina, and Robert Rauschenberg, from Port Arthur, Texas. Varnedoe's warm endorsement helped elevate Twombly, from Lexington, Virginia, to nearly the same level. The problem is that these artists have lived and worked chiefly in Italy or downtown Manhattan, and that their work—abstract, runic, cerebral—betrays little Southern influence to the layman's naked eye. Good old boys they are not.

Varnedoe's eye, of course, was no layman's, and the Southern accents in his own work are never hard to find. His simile for Alberto Giacometti's irony—"as earthy as the slouch of a loping hound"—leaves me grinning conspiratorially. Only a Southerner with Kirk's discernment, eloquence, and tenacity could ever have sold this worldly trio back to the home folks, or sold them to anyone as Dixie's darlings. He's on record with a theory about Twombly—that Civil War–saturated Lexington, with its monuments and sites sacred to Lee and Stonewall Jackson, had turned the artist toward military mythology and paintings like the series "50 Days at Ilium." No one questions that armed ghosts haunt the South. Jasper Johns took his first name from a Revolutionary War hero, Sgt. William Jasper, whose statue stands in a Savannah square. Johns painted American flags and maps of America, and his stepfather was named Robert E. Lee. But that's pretty thin, and Rauschenberg's Southern echoes seem thinner.

Varnedoe's last email, a week before his death, promised me a couple of sentences of insight into this pet project. They never came, of course, and I've been looking for clues ever since. Most helpful was another of his former students, Jeffrey Weiss, curator of modern art at the National Gallery. Weiss said that Kirk had spoken of "a shared language" of art that the three artists developed (they worked, lived, and sometimes slept together in several combinations), a language based in part on their shared experience of Southern culture.

Even the most illustrious career leaves much undone, much unsaid. Taking advantage of the unrestrained hospitality of Varnedoe's sister, Comer Meadows, I made a respectful pilgrimage to Savannah. Touring the famous squares, I encountered Sgt. Jasper and a dozen houses connected to Kirk's family, branches of which have been prominent in the city for centuries. I stayed in the rambling beach cottage on Tybee Island, I ate oysters with Kirk's brother Gordon at the Crab Shack. I walked through the ancestral hunting cabin, now decomposing in the pinewoods. I saw the big brick house on the square where he grew up, and portraits of Johnny Unitas and Ray Charles he drew when he was a boy. We stood on the bluff where a few bricks remain of the family's last "big house," Beaulieu, which burned in 2001.

And finally, the Varnedoe gravesites, under a huge live oak smothered in Spanish moss, on a bluff overlooking the river and the salt marshes. Deep South with all the trimmings—scenes from *Midnight in the Garden of Good and Evil* were filmed just down the river. Several graves are flying Confederate battle flags, and nearby is a headstone for Kirk's cousin, Braxton Bragg Comer.

The footprints end there, light-years from that museum on 53rd Street in Manhattan. All in all, a Southerner's life that showed a fine disregard for the rules and managed to change a few. Maybe it's not too grand to recycle Jasper Johns's epitaph for Marcel Duchamp: "He has changed the condition of being here."

JESSE WINCHESTER

The Tennessee Kid

PHOTOGRAPHS CAN MISLEAD, and sometimes conceal much more than they reveal. But on occasion, usually in hindsight, a photograph radiates so much insight you need sunglasses to examine it. A photograph in my college yearbook, circa 1962, shows a bunch of mugging freshmen engaged in the lame freshman humor that coat-and-tie group portraits traditionally provoked. Two turkeys in the back row are holding up a sign pilfered from a diner somewhere: "One Golden Brown Juicy Breast—with all the trimmings—89 cents."

Standing next to them, his torso half obscured by the juicy breast sign and a very strained look on his face, is a freshman from Memphis named James Ridout Winchester. You have to look carefully to confirm what you know for sure in hindsight, that it isn't Jimmy Winchester's hand holding up the left end of the breast sign. His hands appear to be deep in his pockets, and the sick look on his face says clearly, "Who are these people, and where am I, and why?" And this was in September, long before one of the six-month Siberian winters that drove more than one Southerner to transfer to Tulane.

It might be an understatement to say that Winchester was never comfortable at Williams College. Though a good fraternity welcomed him—he was a Tennessee thoroughbred with a pedigree that included Robert E. Lee—classmates never saw much of Jimmy. He was up in Bennington entertaining bohemian girls with blues chords, or he was on the road with his band, or rehearsing a rockabilly combo deep in the basement of the student union (if you sat quietly in the snack bar, you could just feel the beat). He lived off-campus with a divorced woman. Four years later, Winchester's senior yearbook photograph shows much longer hair and a still-quizzical expression. Beneath it, no honors or activities are listed, though one of the class musicians Jimmy used to play with listed a band called Roget and the Mojo Teeth.

Winchester wasn't the only one who experienced alienation in the Berkshire Mountains of New England. My hillbilly homesickness yielded slightly to an appetite for dead poets and distilled spirits, not necessarily in that order. From the beginning it was music that enabled Winchester to water his roots and endure his exile.

He was from Memphis—a major South Memphis thoroughfare is Winchester Road—and most of us lacked the musical sophistication to grasp a fraction of what that implied. Elvis to be sure, but also Beale Street, B. B. King, Bobby "Blue" Bland, Sam Phillips and Sun Records, Booker T and the MGs. W. C. Handy was still living in Memphis when Jim Winchester was a teenager. When Handy died in 1958, Winchester's grandfather spoke at his funeral.

It was an unfair advantage. Where I grew up, live music was Salty Austin and the Allegheny Ridgerunners, aping Porter Wagoner. On weekdays Salty sold Electrolux vacuum cleaners door-to-door and left personalized guitar picks instead of calling cards. Once a month at American Legion Post 808, an emaciated, Baptist-looking woman named Audrey performed standards on the Hammond organ, backed up by her husband Pike, who looked anesthetized and played the drums with brushes. The culture gap between Sam Phillips and the Audrey/Pike ensemble might account for the discrepancy between Winchester's musical achievements and my own. But probably not.

"My mother tells me music was always my focus," Winchester recalled in 1999. "I studied piano all through grade school and high school, and I was always in a band with my friends, and I played the organ in church. But really, looking back, I always wanted to play guitar in an R&B band."

Going his own way, Winchester became a man of mystery at the college, the kind classmates tend to mythologize. I remember the rumors that he was in Boston or Springfield most weekends, opening shows for Taj Mahal. But a year out of Williams, after graduate study in Germany and a summer playing lounge piano in Memphis, Winchester took his myth to another level. His Vietnam draft notice came and he decamped for Montreal, guitar in hand—the only draft resister in the class, to my knowledge, who took the high road of emigration and public opposition to the war. The "Tennessee kid," as he calls himself in the classic "Brand New Tennessee Waltz," had committed himself to an exile that was neither academic nor symbolic.

"I was so young and naive that it wasn't that difficult a decision," he said later. "I just wasn't thinking very far into the future."

The alumni grapevine works fast those first few years out of school. Winchester's departure was much discussed in New York. Most of us admired him for it. A couple of years after he moved to Montreal, a postcard of sorts arrived, a here's-how-I'm-doing that was characteristically original and myth-enriching. Jim was "Jesse Winchester" now, and that was the name of his debut album on the Bearsville label, produced by Robbie Robertson of The Band. *Jesse Winchester* introduced "The Brand New Tennessee Waltz," "Yankee Lady," and "Biloxi," three of the prettiest, subtlest, most mind-adhesive songs in the country-rock canon. They've been covered by so many singers that they covered a lifetime of alimony payments, as Jesse once told me mournfully.

The album photographs revealed that Jesse had a beard now and a lot more hair—quite a few of us had acquired beaucoup hair in the four years since graduation. He looked like a prophet; he had Robbie Robertson, Garth Hudson, and Levon Helm for sidemen on his album; he knew Bob Dylan and Leonard Cohen. While his fraternity brothers were trying to pass their orals or make junior partner—while I was reviewing TV shows—Jesse was an international fugitive and a Canadian celebrity. He was light years ahead of the pack. And his songs were grand, to my ear—lyrical, ironic, simultaneously self-illuminating and self-deprecating. Smart, and full of displaced-Southerner angst.

"Now you know what they say about snowflakes," he mourns in "Snow," as another iron winter closes in. "How there ain't no two the same? Well, all them flakes look alike to me. Every one is a dirty shame."

Jesse Winchester backed up a wistful personal narrative with everything a boy soaked up in Memphis—blues, R&B, gospel, country, rock, and rockabilly. Critics were uniformly impressed; performers and industry professionals were enthusiastic.

"As a collection of songs, the album is still nearly without peer," Herb Bowie wrote in an online review of Jesse's recordings, thirty-four years later.

"There was an intimacy in those songs that was new," recalls Barry Poss of Sugar Hill Records, which released two later Winchester albums (*Humor Me* in 1988 and *Gentleman of Leisure* in 1999). "It was a whole different take on love and loss."

"What my songs seem mainly to focus on is relationships with women or relationships with God," Winchester told an interviewer. "I tend to get those two confused."

Schoolmates who barely knew Jesse at Williams were suddenly his disciples. If his albums made small waves in the music industry, they made big ones in the class of '66. It's hard to invest much in the celebrity of adults we knew when they were children; we know them too well to buy into the mystique. But the separateness that Jesse always maintained—that was his trademark—allowed us to be his fans. There was a strange meeting in the late '70s that I always recall when I reflect on the paradox of celebrity. I went to hear Jesse play at The Pier in Raleigh, in the company of his old fraternity brother Bill Bennett, who was later to become Secretary of Education and federal drug czar under Ronald Reagan—and eventually the self-appointed guardian of America's morals, until a hemorrhaging addiction to high-stakes gambling cost him his pulpit.

Bennett, too, is a great character, of a less endearing variety. The three of us sat backstage after Jesse's show, in a tiny dressing room that reeked of cigarettes, making awkward small talk about undergraduate adventures. Bennett and I were unconditionally impressed with Winchester; for his part he was impeccably gracious but seemed to find us almost as bewildering as those freshmen with the juicy breast sign in 1962. Bennett and I were both becoming pontificators—of radically different types, I hope—and Jesse was an artist born, a different animal. I know what I think of Bennett; I'm fairly sure I know what Winchester thought of him, too. I had no idea what Jesse thought of me.

There's a distinct male pecking order where musicians rule; you're tone-deaf if you think William Bennett, who once aspired to the presidency of the United States, was the celebrity in that little room. Bennett himself would never make that claim. Like me, like the rest of us, he probably followed the rest of Jesse's career as avidly as Memphis kids followed Elvis.

It's been an uneven, almost unclassifiable career. Winchester became a Canadian citizen in 1973. When Jimmy Carter pardoned the Vietnam draft resisters in 1977, a friend called Jesse in Canada, and he remembers that he "just sat down on the bed and wept, I was so moved." But he kept faith with the Maple Leaf, with the country that welcomed him when America had no peaceful use for him. He lived most of his adult life in Quebec and raised three children there, for years in the Eastern Townships, seventy hard winter miles from Montreal.

Though no less an authority than Bob Dylan calls him one of the best singer-songwriters of his generation—Dylan's generation—the conventional wisdom is that exile deprived Jesse of a chance to be a star.

"His early inability to tour in the U.S. may have permanently stunted his commercial success," speculated Herb Bowie. Jesse's stock never traded briskly on the celebrity exchange; *People* magazine, a founder of that grim exchange, said of Winchester in February of 1989, "He certainly seems too obscure for a performer of his talent."

In 1990 Jesse announced his retirement as a performer and recorded nothing for a decade. When he returned in 1999 with Sugar Hill's *Gentleman of Leisure*, his obscurity had become a theme. In a piece headed "The Return of Jesse Winchester" in the *Toronto Star*, Nick Krewen described an artist "whose stature, through ten albums and 28 years has always been more satellite than star, orbiting the peripheral [*sic*] between respectability and reverence."

"Album sales have been nominal," Krewen added.

Jesse himself made black humor of his meager renown, with a streak of self-mockery prefigured by his second album, *Third Down, 110 to Go*. He recalled opening for Jimmy Buffett and singing one of his own songs that Buffett had recorded. "The audience was annoyed because they thought I was singing one of Jimmy's songs," he said. "It's kind of the story of my life."

The image industry isn't everything—in an age of Britney Spears, Donald Trump, and *American Idol* it's a pretty dismal business. While his career appeared to languish, Winchester's songs were recorded by a formidable lineup of discriminating A-list artists including Joan Baez, the Everly Brothers, Waylon Jennings, Bonnie Raitt, Emmylou Harris, Reba McEntire, Elvis Costello, and Wynonna Judd. The attention dried up but not the money. Unlike some great blues artists who had more lean years than fat, Winchester never had to load trucks or play lodge picnics to make ends meet. But he became one of those cult figures who separates serious music buffs from the day-trippers. Everyone knowledgeable knew *who* he was, but almost no one knew *where* he was.

By paying close attention I managed several Winchester sightings over the years, every one rewarding. One night in the mid-'80s my wife and I caught up with him at Rhythm Alley in Chapel Hill, NC, for a set highlighted by a remarkable live version of Jesse's funky "Rhumba Man." ("My step might be old-fashioned / But it's just fine with me / I got a couple of rhumba steps / You might like to see.")

Here was a skinny, incongruously formal guy with a neatly trimmed beard, dressed like an off-duty librarian, performing a weird soft-shoe shuffle like your Uncle Dan might assay after his third martini. But you quickly saw the art of it. No hoofer, no athlete, Winchester just had those Beale Street rhythms coiled around his bones, and his exhibition of fancy footwork was one of the most arresting novelties in show business. If you're thinking Savion Glover, move along. If you love the Rabbit Dance performed by Too Slim of Riders in the Sky—who also played Rhythm Alley—"Rhumba Man" live might have been your personal epiphany.

Backstage alone, reserved as always but with his Southern manners fine-tuned by the presence of a lady, Jesse seemed genuinely glad to see us. The last time I talked to him, he was working my favorite bluegrass festival, Doc Watson's MerleFest in North Wilkesboro, NC. With all the credentials he carried—Memphis, Montreal, Nashville, political dissent, the imprimatur of Dylan and The Band—you'd think Jesse might have worked up some kind of hip look for himself, at least onstage, at least surrounded by so many musicians in their righteous gear. Instead he performed in a V-neck sweater, striped button-down shirt, chinos, and penny loafers—a uniquely retro costume borrowed from a small-town history teacher, or one of our more conservative preppies at Williams long ago.

Graying now, playing alone on a vintage guitar, Jesse made our day—the few of us, the ones who knew—with a low-key set of familiar, beautifully crafted songs. Backstage he was abstracted, shy, a wayfaring stranger who didn't seem to know anyone—still an exile, as he sang and wrote, "with my feet in Dixie and my head in the cool blue North."

The class grapevine is fraying now; there are a lot of missing links in the network, one way or another. Classmates have died, of course; another one reached Jesse by email to ask him if he might be interested in performing at the fortieth reunion of the class of 1966. The predictable answer was a polite but resounding "No thanks." Not even Barry Poss, who recorded Jesse, could ever tell me exactly where to find him, though he knew people who might know, he said. The only clues were on Jesse's website. Once it listed a three-show tour in Northern California—Petaluma (McNear's Mystic Theater), Saratoga, Santa Cruz—that coincided exactly with a trip I made to Death Valley. But those east-west roads in the desert aren't so good, and I felt way too old to drive across the Sierra Nevadas at night, even to see Jesse Winchester. There was no hurry, it seemed to me. The Rhumba Man was out there somewhere, and somewhere we'd meet again. I was wrong. In 2014 I got a call from a friend in New York, a classmate who had once played the drums in Jesse's band. His news was that Winchester, back in the States since 2002, had died of cancer at his home in Charlottesville, just short of his seventieth birthday. I thought of some lines from "The Brand New Tennessee Waltz": "Have all of your passionate violins play a tune for a Tennessee kid / who's feeling like leaving another town, with no place to go if he did / 'Cause they'll catch you wherever you're hid."

ANNE BRADEN

An Embarrassing Woman

Traveling about the South today, distributing the doctrine of totalitarian
government, is a husband-wife team by name of Carl and Anne Braden.
—Rep. Dale Alford (D-Arkansas), 1959

The battle has always been a battle for the hearts and minds of white people.
The fight against racism is our issue. It's not something that we're called on
to help people of color with. We need to become involved with it as if
our lives depended on it because really, in truth, they do.
—Anne Braden: 1924–2006

R EADERS HAVE OBSERVED, sometimes humorously, that I often
write essays inspired or influenced by obituaries. If chronic
morbidity is involved, let psychiatrists explain it. The part I
understand is that a life ended is a story that won't be revised or

radically refocused; I can praise or damn the deceased with little fear that the best of them will yet disappoint me, or the worst surprise me. I can hope, in other words, to do justice to them, and offer them confidently as examples.

The other reason, I know, is that the people I admire most are embarrassing people—outlaws, agitators, uncompromising rebels, and crusaders whose courage makes the rest of us uncomfortable. During their lives we write about them less than we should, perhaps, because most journalists affect a detachment that distances them from the champions of lost and quixotic causes. Then one of them dies and guilt seizes me. In one sense it's too late. But it's never pointless to pay your last respects to heroes, to settle scores with history and place their accomplishments in the context they deserve. The truly embarrassing people, Martin Luther King, Jr., for instance—or Jesus Christ—can be a greater force dead than alive.

Anne Braden, who died March 6, 2006, in Louisville, KY, was one of the most embarrassing Southern women who ever lived. Braden was ostracized and reviled as Louisville's greatest embarrassment for fifty years, as a result of one of those grotesque miscarriages of justice that every Southerner would like to forget—and most of them do, with alarming success.

In May 1954—the same week that the Supreme Court's decision in *Brown v. Board of Education* changed the South forever—Braden and her husband Carl bought a house in a white suburb of Louisville and turned it over to a black couple, the Wades, who were challenging the city's unwritten code of residential segregation. The Louisville of the '50s was a cosmopolitan city with one of the South's most liberal newspapers, the *Courier-Journal* (the Bradens were reporters for its sister paper, the *Times*), and a reputation for racial moderation. But this was its darkest hour. After a cross-burning on the lot next door failed to drive off the Wades, half the house was destroyed by dynamite, from a charge set off under their daughter's bedroom.

No one was injured, but when Louisville's embarrassment reached a flash point, the Commonwealth's attorney turned not on the bombers and cross-burners, never apprehended, but on the Bradens. They were indicted for sedition—conspiring to incite civil unrest—under a long-neglected law passed during a previous Red scare in 1920. Playing to the anticommunist hysteria orchestrated by Sen. Joseph McCarthy and his House Un-American Activities Committee (HUAC), the state prosecuted Carl Braden, a journalist active in progressive politics, as a virtual Soviet agent. In a verdict that defies comprehension for anyone who missed the fun of the '50s, Braden was convicted of sedition and sentenced to fifteen years in prison.

As happened so often in those days, when higher courts surveyed Southern jurisprudence, the conviction was overturned and Braden released after seven months in prison. Anne Braden's case never came to trial. Louisville, struggling like other Southern cities with the court-ordered integration of its schools, tried to forget the Bradens and, in the contemporary idiom, "move on." But the Bradens refused to let Louisville forget them. The Wades and other white progressives who had helped them found life easier elsewhere; the easy life never appealed to Carl and Anne Braden. Now unemployable by mainstream newspapers, they remained in the city as professional activists and committed the rest of their lives to civil rights, civil liberties, antiwar and antinuclear protests, and every labor and environmental cause that might make the establishment uncomfortable. With the Old-Left Southern Conference Educational Fund and its newsletter, the *Southern Patriot*, as their base, the Bradens set off to fight the South's uphill battles for social justice side by side.

They lost and lost, in the beginning, and even endured a second collision with Kentucky's arcane sedition law in 1967, when they were indicted for protesting strip mining in Eastern Kentucky. But the law was declared unconstitutional that year, and as the civil rights movement gained momentum, the Bradens began to see some of their lost causes prevail.

W. G. Sebald and Primo Levi, among many of the significant writers of the terrifying twentieth century, agree that responsible writers and responsible citizens share a primary moral imperative to fight amnesia and amnesiacs. To forget, they emphasize, is to commit a second sin against the victims and the heroes, against those who suffered and those who resisted. It's a warning that can't be repeated too often in the American South. Sick of being patronized by outsiders and foreigners, Southerners—this one included—often remind hypocritical Yankees that the Northern states also bred millions of harsh racists, some of them violent, and that many Northern cities are still as segregated as the old Jim Crow South. This is indisputably true. But it was mostly in the South, as the Bradens' miseries remind us, that the worst racial attitudes were indulged and protected by the courts and by public officials. The local judiciary offered more protection to night riders than to the people they terrorized. In the Southern states we not only practiced the unspeakable but codified and institutionalized it.

"Segregation gripped the minds of many Southerners like a chronic disease, an incurable addiction," John Egerton wrote in *Speak Now Against the Day*. "In their fervor for it, some whites would prove themselves ready to ride it down to defeat, just as their forebears had ridden slavery."

To read *Subversive Southerner*, Catherine Fosl's 2002 biography of Anne Braden, is to be reminded of many things we may have forgotten, deliberately or carelessly. My own flawed memory is not exempted. I'd forgotten or never adequately registered much of the psychotically irrational rhetoric that turned the Cold War's Red scares against the labor and civil rights movements. To many Southerners of the McCarthy era, a "communist" was anyone who threatened the status quo, and the careers of segregationists like Jesse Helms were based entirely on this outrageous conflation. I once wrote that the Cold War and Jim Crow were the twin "pole stars" of Jesse's life. I see now that they were one and the same star. Sometimes logic blinds us to the obvious. Crushing domestic dissent by equating it with treason in a war climate—familiar once again since 9-11—has always been the Far Right's most devastating strategy.

Many Southerners still respond to politicians who pander to amnesia and comforting illusions about the past. A poor memory is the best cure for a troubled conscience—read Sen. Helms's 2005 memoir. But for every lapse of memory, for every dose of political Ambien, there has always been a native conscience-twister like

Anne Braden to ring their doorbells and disturb their sleep. As she described it in her memoir of the Wade case, *The Wall Between* (1958), the somnolent South of the '50s was a kind of police state—and an especially ugly one because the Bull Connors with their nightsticks were reinforced by the implicit threat of vigilante violence.

It was the worst of times. An established order based on flagrant, entrenched, oppressive injustice brings out the worst in ordinary people—apathy, cowardice, cruelty, every kind of self-serving and self-protecting herd behavior. But in the best, oppression always brings out the best.

There were never more than a handful, but they were the best, the hope, the flowers of the South—of the homeland that treated them, for most of their lives, like noxious weeds. Anne Braden, a slight, soft-spoken, deceptively fragile-looking woman with a slow Deep South drawl, discovered that persecution only stiffened her spine and stoked her indignation. Once the '60s had given her a brief taste of victory, nothing could stop her; in her seventies they described her as "the rebel without a pause." Bred to be a Southern lady in Anniston, AL, a graduate of Virginia's exclusive Randolph-Macon College, she traded country clubs, charities, and bridge groups for courtrooms, jails, and detention pens. While other couples saved to send their children to college, the Bradens sent their three children to live with grandparents while they served time and raised money to make bail. When her husband died prematurely in 1975, Braden steeled herself with a line from a song by Joe Hill: "Don't mourn, organize."

Freedom and *justice* are tall words with wide shoulders that make most people uneasy. She was never afraid of them, or of much else either. Just reading about Anne Braden makes you ashamed if you ever pulled a punch in a fight against injustice—and certain that you must have. And she had farther to travel than most of us, to get to the light that sustained her. My father stalked out of a faculty lounge when an odious (Yankee) racist called Dr. King, a few hours dead, "a rabble-rouser"; policing his children's language, he judged the N-word more obscene than the F-word. Braden's father, a feed merchant, once said in her presence, "We ought to have a good lynching every once in a while to keep the nigger in his place."

This man's daughter became the white person black leaders trusted above all others. Martin Luther King, Jr., praised her integrity in his "Letter from Birmingham Jail"; Fred Shuttlesworth was an intimate friend; and Angela Davis wrote the foreword for her biography ("a legend . . . her deep commitment to the South was and remains the major theme around which she has forged her identity"). Jesse Jackson writes on its dust jacket, "She spent her life fighting to build a New South, where all our people could live together in freedom and equality."

But even for her black allies, Braden could be an embarrassment. Utterly convinced of her loyalty, they had to be wary of her reputation. The "communist" smear, from the early years of relentless Red-baiting, would always haunt her. Because it was HUAC's mantra, she refused all her life to answer the question, "Are you now or have you ever been a member of the Communist Party?" The refusal, just as HUAC designed it, fed the old paranoia. Biracial organizations that recruited from the moderate middle class accepted Braden's help but rarely advertised it. As a consequence some histories omit her or give her less credit than she deserves. Even *Speak Now Against the Day*, John Egerton's magisterial tribute to Southerners who fought segregation in the silent decades before the Movement, ends with *Brown v. Board of Education* in 1954, when the Bradens' story was just beginning. They're mentioned only in an epilogue.

The road of high principle was never paved with accolades; credit, praise, and prizes are peripheral to the life of the conscience. By her own account Braden got everything she required from the life she chose, and more. Late honors, which came in her seventies, she regarded ironically. She marched to a tune written by another distinguished and stiff-necked Kentuckian, Wendell Berry: "You can best serve civilization by being against what usually passes for it."

Outside her political subculture—"the beloved community" of progressive activists she joined in the '50s and for the most part outlived—Braden remained an acute and glorious embarrassment. The fearful never forgive the fearless for exposing their limitations. There's a revisionist myth that it was the diplomats, "the bridge-builders"—the gradualists—who deserved the real credit for breaking down the color barriers in the South. I never heard Anne Braden laugh out loud, but I can imagine it. If we'd left Jim Crow in the custody of the gradualists, we'd still be bending over separate drinking fountains.

God bless the agitators, the subversives and troublemakers, the extremists, the bleeding hearts, the lonely believers in moral imperatives, the awkwardly and dangerously ahead of their time. Sometimes when these fierce warriors leave the stage, their well-meaning but compromised fellow travelers breathe a sigh of relief. But when the dust has settled, they were the ones who made all the difference. They were the best of the South, then and now, and "the cream of America," as Anne Braden called her comrades in arms. The American experiment has ended when our milk runs too thin for any more of that cream to rise.

TOMMY THOMPSON

The Last Song of Father Banjo

T
OMMY THOMPSON WAS from West Virginia, and he bore a certain resemblance to a mountain, or at least to someone who'd just come down from the mountain after talking to the Boss. He wore the weather on his shoulders.

"Tommy could close down the light and bring on the night," said his second wife, Cece Conway, recalling the storms that rolled down the mountain. But when his sun was shining, birds broke into song and branches into blossom. After his final performance, well into his fatal illness, he called Conway and told her, "I have a sunny disposition—even still I guess."

She doesn't deny it. Tommy Thompson, the huge man his friends called Father Banjo and the Cajuns dubbed "Uncle Wide Load," died in January 2012 at sixty-five, after nearly a decade of silent decline with an Alzheimer's-related dementia. Though he'd been off the stage for so long, and virtually beyond communication for several years, the response to his death defined the critical difference between the weightless thing called celebrity and the rare personality that actually alters other people's lives.

"He was a wonder in many different ways," said his longtime piano player, writer Bland Simpson. "People would seek Tommy out—older, younger, men, women—to tell him, 'I play music because of you.' He imparted the love of music and inspired people. That's magic."

United by a fear that he might have died forgotten or underrated, friends, scholars, and musicians fell over each other trying to explain Tommy Thompson. It would have delighted and amused him. Tommy was not so much a humble man as a compulsively reflective one, a philosopher by training and inclination—possibly the only entertainer who ever claimed the seminal influence of both Ludwig Wittgenstein and Uncle Dave Macon. He took the long view.

"He was the philosophical graduate student always surrounding himself with unanswerable questions," recalled mandolinist Bertram Levy. "But when he got the banjo, it set him free."

In a cover story for the *Old-Time Herald*, written six months before Thompson's death, David Potorti collected a treasury of reminiscences by Tommy's musical collaborators. It's important to note that the Red Clay Ramblers, the band Thompson fathered and anchored for twenty-two years, must have the highest aggregate IQ and the most university degrees of any string band that ever lived. We might all covet eulogists like these. The quote that sticks with me is from Mike Craver, the Ramblers' original piano man.

"I remember watching him and thinking, if I had to describe a Shakespearean character, it would be Tommy. He was big then, and he had that kind of Falstaff quality to him—red hair, and a red beard. He was amazing looking, and the word that comes to mind is probably charismatic. You looked at him, and you had to look back, because he had such a presence, he just exuded this personality."

Thompson was "amazing looking." More antique even than "Shakespearean," his was an Old Testament look, like Goliath in bronze armor or Ezekiel in a dusty sheepskin. He looked that way, and he was bigger and smarter and spoke in a lower register than almost anyone, and he could play the banjo like the devil himself. And none of that fully explains his singularity. The elegant lyrics of "Hot Buttered Rum"—a Thompson song I often hum or whistle—capture the essence of the man I knew because they're both cynical and sentimental, side by side.

"It's always seemed to me a slight irony that a man of Tommy's breadth and genius didn't become very famous," said folklorist Henry Glassie. "I think he should have. Tommy wrote some of the finest songs of the genre of his period. In some ways, Tommy will probably be forgotten and his songs will be remembered."

It isn't that Thompson performed in obscurity, or that show business disappointed him. From *Diamond Studs* off-Broadway in 1975 to Broadway's *Fool Moon* in 1993, his credits for musical theater as an actor, musician, composer, and arranger would have made several careers for a less expansive talent. Two of the Ramblers' great supporters have been Sam Shepard and Garrison Keillor, and thanks to their patronage Tommy Thompson probably enjoyed more national exposure than any banjo player besides John Hartford. The Ramblers' music was featured on Keillor's *Prairie Home Companion*, in Shepard's film *Far North*, and on TV shows including *Northern Exposure* and *Ryan's Hope*. Thompson and company were the onstage band for Shepard's Broadway play *A Lie of the Mind*, and featured players in his motion picture *Silent Tongue*.

For a decade or more the Ramblers were in evidence everywhere, including Eastern Europe, the Middle East, and Africa, on tours sponsored by the USIA. But a dozen fine CDs made no one rich, and in the music business that's the single measure of celebrity. Thompson was a connoisseur's musician, a stylist who took on the mountain masters and won the World Champion Old Time Banjo Contest at Union Grove, NC, in 1971. The Ramblers were a connoisseur's band, only with some wires loose. Their irreverent eclecticism—they all wrote songs in different styles—eventually moved them beyond the protection of every established genre.

What began as a traditional string band, rooted in mountain fiddle tunes and superb instrumentation—"a band that might have existed in 1930, but didn't"—evolved into an act that journalists struggled to describe. "A fantasy roadhouse band from a vanished rural America" was the *New York Times*' best effort. When Sam Shepard cast them as a raffish, impudent medicine-show band in *Silent Tongue*, it was less a performance than a Rambler self-portrait.

Even after Hollywood, Broadway, and the African odyssey ("Regions of Rain" is Tommy's ultimate road song), the Ramblers were proudly and thoroughly a local band. It was in Chapel Hill, NC, that they went to college or first met Father Banjo, resident master of the clawhammer and the categorical imperative.

In Chapel Hill the Ramblers and their faithful are not so much a cult as an extended family, with the closest family ties. A Ramblers concert was not an entertainment option but a seasonal celebration, like Mardi Gras or the Blessing of the Fleet in a fishing village. Everyone came—everyone with musical tastes to the populist side of Rachmaninoff—and everyone who could play wanted to play with the Ramblers. There were memorable nights when nearly everyone did. That atmosphere prevailed at Tommy's funeral. The service, a high-church Episcopalian affair with bells and incense, might have surprised the unchurched mountain Christian in the coffin. But upstairs in the parish hall afterwards, a dozen-deep string band—led by folklorist Alan Jabbour, the protean John McCutcheon, and original Ramblers Jim Watson and Bill Hicks—re-created the anarchic splendor of the vintage Ramblers when Father Banjo was in his prime.

Thompson was always the big man at the center, at the hammering heart of the music. How it must have stunned him, still in early middle age, when the music started to fade. But the performance I remember best created a quiet place where his deep voice cast a spell and his banjo rang pure as a church bell. *The Last Song of*

John Proffit, a one-man show he wrote and created in its entirety, could stand as his own last will and testament.

His portrait of a nineteenth-century minstrel was a powerful piece of theater, charged with the passion and insight of a thoughtful man who'd been brooding and waiting a long time to take center stage in the spotlight, alone. Two St. Louis reviewers compared him to Mark Twain. Tommy was a riveting actor, with his stubborn streak of darkness and enough gravitas for the College of Cardinals.

And for once he was alone. Thompson's ego was so welltempered that he'd always worked with an ensemble—a formidable ensemble. Talent aside, if you've never seen core Ramblers Jack Herrick, Clay Buckner, and Chris Frank, well, they're not physical types you find every day in the coffee line at Starbucks. In such company, even Mount Thompson wasn't always the first thing to catch your eye. The Yoda-like Buckner, the most effortlessly funny man who ever made a fiddle cry, was responsible for "Father Banjo"—as in "Speak to us, Father Banjo. Read to us from the Book of Gigs."

Tommy wore his learning lightly, and covertly in the company of old-time pickers who entertain no excessive respect for books. He was alert to the condescension of people who take string-band musicians for grade-school dropouts, rarely yielding to the urge to embarrass them. He was easy in the most literate company. One of his best friends away from music was the Pulitzer Prize–winning poet Henry Taylor, whose intimidating erudition has shamed everyone who knows him, including me.

Taylor never scared Tommy. It was at the poet's house on the

Outer Banks that we had—in retrospect—a first foreshadowing of the illness that was gathering its forces to bring the big man down. We'd been drinking a little. After dark six or seven of us walked out to the beach to look at the stars; one of my jokes was calling Tommy "Ursa Major." We took to singing, and after the amateurs exhausted their repertoire we turned to Tommy to keep us going—a man who in his time must have known a thousand songs. He sang one song, fumbled the lyrics of a second, and then fell silent.

The evening was fairly young, and we thought it was just a mood, another cold front moving across his internal weather map. This was a year before the first symptoms of dementia were diagnosed. Tommy's last song that night wasn't one of his own—I never heard him sing his own songs in a social setting. It was one of his favorites, an ancient standard he sang in *John Proffit*: "Hard Times Come Again No More."

EUBIE BLAKE

A Century of Ragtime

MANY YEARS AGO — at least twenty — when I was a very young man taking myself seriously in New York, some friends took me to a jazz performance at the Overseas Press Club, a benefit for something or other. It was an important black musician, Thelonious Monk, I think. I can't recall for certain. There were a lot of celebrities and media big shots in the audience. Just before the first note a bunch of people came in with a very old black man, not supporting him exactly — he looked fairly spry — but surrounding him on all sides so he couldn't bruise himself on anything or fall more than a few inches in any direction. The old man looked amused.

"God, that's Eubie Blake," said a man in the next row. "I think he played with Scott Joplin. He must be a hundred years old."

None of us had ever heard of Eubie Blake, a ragtime pianist and composer who retired before we were born. But about seven years later, when a man from the QRS Music Roll Company called my newspaper and asked me to send the music critic down to interview Eubie Blake, I remembered the night at the Press Club and reserved the assignment for myself. It isn't every day you get to meet a 107-year-old musician.

It turned out that Eubie was only ninety-one, still active and in the middle of a comeback. QRS, the only surviving manufacturer of player piano rolls in the United States, was hoping to cash in on the ragtime revival by getting Eubie to repunch the master rolls he'd cut for the company in 1912, the year my grandfather graduated from college. The rolls were getting a little ragged after sixty years, but luckily the original artist was still available to update them.

It was a perfect setup, the ragtime equivalent of having Arthur Rubinstein come and play in your parlor. A bright winter afternoon, a beautiful old red-brick factory, Eubie sitting in the sunshine beneath a fifteen-foot window at the enormous recording piano that must have been at least as old as he was. He played off and on for three hours for an audience of five—his wife, QRS president Ramsi Tick, one technician, my photographer, and me. I felt guilty about the critic I didn't bring along, a man who understood the music and its history. Eubie had to explain syncopation to me and demonstrate it repeatedly before I began to catch on. He must have wondered why they sent him a musical illiterate. But Eubie Blake live was as much a visual as a musical experience, and I told myself that a tone-deaf film critic might appreciate some details that the man with the good ear would have missed.

You could start with the artist's skull. No hair had grown there in the twentieth century, as ancient photographs attest. The skin that caught the sunlight had acquired a kind of permanence, a metallic sheen that seemed to have nothing to do with human flesh. Eubie's head looked like a priceless bronze, a Tang dynasty heirloom that a loving curator removed from its glass case and polished till it burned.

It was the second most arresting thing about him. The legendary hands with their twelve-key span really had to be seen up close—I sat on the same piano bench—to be believed. Twelve keys is almost a foot, a couple of inches more than any other pianist could manage. The fingers weren't only supernaturally long but bizarrely spatulate, as if nine decades of pounding keyboards had flattened them almost to the bone. I have to invoke E.T. to give you a real image of those fingers. But it seems insulting to Eubie to yoke the mechanical darling of a single season with the human achievement of a century. It's enough to say that the nature of ragtime piano is to play a syncopated melody with one hand and a regularly accented accompaniment with the other, and that with another twenty years' practice Eubie Blake might have played them both with the same hand.

At ninety the weird fingers still moved as fast as he asked them to, and they weren't the only things that moved. Ragtime isn't

sitting-still music, and he rarely sat still when he played. When
he felt he was getting hot he'd stick out his tongue a little and
bounce up and down and back and forth on the bench, the bony
old body looking frail enough to break if he came down any harder.
He got hot and cooled off again a half dozen times during his session at QRS. He rarely missed a note. Just once or twice, rest-
ing between songs, his mind would drift a little—once he started
singing "Waitin' for the Robert E. Lee" softly to himself while his
wife was talking—and we'd be reminded that he was older than we
were. And just a year younger than the late Franklin D. Roosevelt.

He and I had rapport, I think—about as much as you're going
to get between a ninety-year-old black man from Baltimore and a
thirty-year-old white man who was born in Nova Scotia. At the age
when Eubie started playing piano in a Baltimore whorehouse, I was
shocking the sixth grade by dropping out of the Methodist Youth
Fellowship. He told me his favorite joke about why black pianists
learned to play ragtime, which relies heavily on the black keys:
"Back in those days there was so much Jim Crow we were afraid
to hit the white ones." He admitted that Scott Joplin might have
had an edge on him as a composer. He told me that neither he nor
Joplin could play the piano like another black man whose name I've
forgotten, a musician with classical training who was forced into
ragtime because America, still fond of its minstrel shows, wasn't
ready for black fingers playing Mozart in Carnegie Hall. When he
talked about the color barrier, which he did freely, it was without
any edge and in the deep past tense.

The only secret of his longevity, Eubie said, was his wife. If she
hadn't taken him in hand he'd have killed himself years ago chasing

skirts and breaking up saloons. He used to be pretty good with his fists, Eubie told me, and held up a fist to show me. I'd never seen a fist made up of eight-inch fingers about as thick as a praying mantis's forearms. I'd have laughed if it hadn't seemed disrespectful. I don't think he was kidding.

When we said good-bye he gave me his card, as if I might need a pianist for some lodge clambake or wedding reception and should give him a call. The card has been in my wallet ever since, along with lawyers' and agents' cards and the cards of people who tried to sell me insurance:

Eubie Blake

Pianist-Arranger

Composer of Shuffle Along & I'm Just Wild About Harry

Lou Leslie's Blackbirds & Memories of You

I wrote a long story that read more like art appreciation than music criticism and made a weak joke, as it seems to me now, about Eubie trying to get the music rolls right because he wasn't sure he'd be around in sixty years to do them again. As if he was obviously on borrowed time. Eubie went on to an astonishing comeback, playing concerts and television with some of the best young musicians in the business. He became twice the legend he'd been when he and his partner Noble Sissle integrated Broadway in 1921. There was a new Broadway musical celebrating Eubie Blake and his music, and he was in the audience opening night. He outlived his wife.

The time came at last when I had to take Eubie's card out of my wallet and file it with the cards that for one reason or another have gone inactive. He hadn't been feeling well enough to attend his birthday party, a lavish celebrity affair at the Kennedy Center. Five days later he died, perhaps of old age. This time he really was one hundred years old.*

Celebrity obituaries aren't an exalted art form. Local columnists often use them to pass along tired myths and to give themselves a little glamour by association. Years ago, when I was writing about films and TV and celebrities on a regular basis, I set down some guidelines for eulogies. I had to have had some personal contact with the deceased, including a moment or two that wasn't shared by other notebook jockeys, and I had to admire the individual a great deal. I went through ten years of articles and columns, and I found only two entertainers who'd qualified: Groucho Marx and Jack Benny.

Fast company. But not too fast for Eubie. I leave his place in history to be decided by other musicians. I just pass along what I was sure of in his company—that he was an authentic American landmark, an irrepressible, indestructible bald-headed package of talent and endurance that doesn't come along even once in a century.

*According to Blake, and the obituary fact-checkers at the New York Times and the news services. But after his death, research turned up documents, including his passport, indicating that he was born in 1887, not 1883. If that was the case he composed his first rag at the age of twelve.

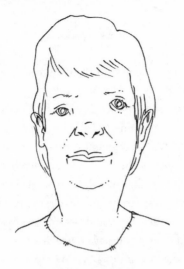

JUDY BONDS

This Land Is Your Land

WHO WILL REPLACE her, who will fill the lace-up workboots worn by Judy Bonds? Whenever a community loses a great talent or a great spirit, eulogists declare affectionately—sometimes truthfully—"There'll never be another one like this one." In the singular case of Judy Bonds, the irrepressible, indefatigable Appalachian crusader who died of cancer in January 2011, it's not only true but ominous. There are people we love and people we respect, but only a handful we desperately need—individuals who occupy a unique place in the political ecosystem and play roles so critical that a democracy, in their absence, is a pale and futile charade.

Such a player, such a presence was Judy Bonds of Whitesville, West Virginia. A coal miner's daughter and a Christian believer, she correctly identified mountaintop removal mining as an abomination and the work of the devil, and devoted her life to the holy cause of opposing it. She was that rarest of Americans, the authentic grassroots resister and organizer, the unwilling, un-silent victim of corporate arrogance and criminal negligence. In the 2010 election cycle the term "corporate feudalism" was prominent. It warned us against becoming a banana republic where cash outweighs every moral consideration, where predatory capitalists assume that people who have less money, or no money, are helpless to resist the will or even the crimes and degeneracy of people who have a great deal. In this post-democratic society the poor are once again feudal serfs and sub-citizens. Power encounters no greater surprise, in an increasingly passive, gullible America, than when it pushes and someone local pushes back.

Someone like Judy Bonds. Where the law is scorned and the landscape devastated by corporate greed on steroids, no one should dismiss the deterrent effect of outside journalists and environmentalists or dedicated young altruists with master's degrees in social work from Columbia (as a hillbilly with a master's from Columbia, I'm not mocking). But "outside agitators," as the bosses have labeled them for a century, are conspicuous and easier to neutralize in an insular world like the coal country of West Virginia and Kentucky. What the bosses fear most and expect least is articulate, organized resistance from their designated victims.

"In Southern West Virginia we live in a war zone," said Judy Bonds. "Three and one-half million pounds of explosives are being used every day to blow up the mountains. Blasting our communities, blasting our homes, poisoning us, trying to intimidate us. I don't mind being poor. I mind being blasted and poisoned. There are no jobs on a dead planet."

I don't think Bill McKibben could have said it more forcefully. The idea of "grassroots" protest has been distorted by the media. The Tea Party is a grassroots movement only in the sense that its members are "common" people, unburdened with wealth or influence. But where the Tea Party is a movement of the deceived and manipulated, a pawn on a big board where real power plays for keeps, Bonds's movement against the mountain-crushing coal bosses is a coalition of the purely *undeceived*. It's the actual voice of the aggrieved and oppressed, at least the ones whose eyes are open.

To understand the importance of a figure like Judy Bonds, as well as the odds stacked against her, you have to try to understand West Virginia. It's an odd place, a mono-economy and an absolute monarchy where King Coal has been enthroned for 150 years. (There's even a town named Odd, near Coal City in Raleigh County. There are also towns named Man, Van, Bim, and Bud, as if the founders declined to waste letters on coal camps that might not last too long.) The Democratic Party has long been dominant, and its U.S. senators, like Jay Rockefeller and the late Robert E. Byrd, have sometimes won the praise of Washington liberals. But not for reigning in the coal industry. In West Virginia Big Coal owns both political parties and nearly all the media. When the activist and novelist Denise Giardina ran for governor in 2000, on a platform denouncing mountaintop removal, she received only 2 percent of the vote. The media were so hostile to Giardina that many voters never realized she was in the race.

That's the world as Judy Bonds found it. Even the churches in Boone County sided with the coal companies, even while the streams ran black, the fish died, strange orange and white deposits in the water were identified as carcinogenic synthetics, and coal dust filled the air until, as Bonds recalled it, "My grandson couldn't hardly breathe." When she protested and threatened to sue Massey Energy, the outlaw coal company designated by environmentalists as "America's scariest polluter," company lawyers laughed at her. When she joined Coal River Mountain Watch, the first group of local activists to stand up to Massey, many of her neighbors shunned, cursed, or threatened her. At least one miner's wife punched her in the head, and her daughter bought her a stun gun to protect herself. "Massey has been able to steal the spine out of people," Bonds said. "It's a lot like battered wives, that Stockholm syndrome, where you identify with your abuser. I've lost a lot of friends over speaking out."

A lot of spine has been stolen up in West Virginia since the Battle of Blair Mountain in 1921, when ten thousand furious miners staged an armed rebellion against the coal bosses and their goons, an uprising that required U.S. Army infantry and Air Force bombers to put down. A lot of mountains have been stolen, too—at least four hundred by recent count, pulverized by Big Coal's explosives and earthmovers. Mixed ironies, sour and sweet, attach themselves to Judy Bonds's death at this particular moment. She was only fifty-eight, and died of a cancer that had spread from her lungs.

Her father, who worked in the mines all his life, died of black lung disease shortly after he retired—but he was sixty-five. It's painful to think that Massey's toxins and coal dust killed her, in the end. If Bonds had lived just a few more days, she could have celebrated the Environmental Protection Agency's decision to revoke the permit for Arch Coal's Spruce No. 1 Mine in Logan County, one of the nation's largest and most heinous mountaintop removal projects. This was a significant victory, the first time the EPA has ever rescinded a clean water permit for a coal mine.

Yet by living until January 3, she managed to outlast—by four days—Massey Energy's nightmare CEO Don Blankenship, whose resignation went into effect December 31, 2010. We assume, we want to believe, that she knew this when she died. Blankenship was Bonds's nemesis, the very man responsible for the dead fish and the grandchildren choking on coal dust. It's tempting to dramatize her entire career as a Manichaean struggle between her light and his darkness. With his jowls and mustache, his beady eyes and curled-lip sneer, Blankenship is a stage villain direct from central casting, more like a character from a Coen brothers' film or a *Saturday Night Live* skit than a flesh-and-blood businessman. "Spit up from hell," as one mountaineer described him, "most likely for cheating the devil at cards." Create a category for individuals who are grasping, callous, and shamelessly, mind-numbingly evil, and in the black hole where that category ends, Don Blankenship begins.

"All in all, Don Blankenship has probably caused more suffering than any other human being in Appalachia," judges Cecil Roberts of the United Mine Workers. The UMW, which once represented

95 percent of West Virginia's coal miners, fought a losing battle against Blankenship's aggressive union-crushing and now enrolls just a quarter of the workforce.

Blankenship may be the only public figure in America whose Wikipedia profile reads as if it was written by his worst enemy, or his ex-wife. Can it be true that he virtually purchased two seats on the West Virginia Supreme Court to overturn a $76 million judgment against him—and got away with it? (At least until he was filmed raising hell on the Riviera with the chief justice and their girlfriends.) That his mines were charged with 4,268 toxic spills and safety violations between 2000 and 2005, against just 800 for the second-worst coal company? That in 2009, the last year before it exploded and killed 29 miners, Massey's mine at Upper Big Branch was charged with 468 safety violations and assessed nearly a million dollars in penalties? That he manhandled his maid and threw food at her? That after one of his mines contaminated his own home drinking water, he had water piped in from another town for himself, and left his neighbors to drink poison? I know it's true that he beat up an ABC News reporter and tried to destroy his camera, because I saw the footage that survived.

This stuff goes on and on—there's no space here to do it justice. Keith Olbermann, humorously, used to feature "The Worst Person in the World" on his news show. In Don Blankenship, we may actually have found that person. Bernie Madoff is serving a life sentence in North Carolina and all he did was steal from the rich—America's most unspeakable crime—for which I might have applauded him if he'd only given some percentage to the poor. How much worse is Blankenship, retired with a golden parachute worth tens of millions, who all but annihilated a whole bio-region, a classic American landscape, a culture, and a way of life? Not even to mention the miners who died because he was ruthless and oblivious.

This was the Goliath, the Darth Vader, the coal-powered Godzilla that Judy Bonds set out to bring down. It was hardly a fair fight. Blankenship had courts, senators, congressmen, governors, newspapers, an $18 million salary to spend, and the scruples of an assassin. Bonds had a storefront office in Whitesville, a $12,000 salary, a little money to travel with—her title at CRMW was out-reach coordinator—and a fighter's heart. During most of her career dueling Massey and mountaintop removal, she faced the fur-ther handicap of a Republican administration that discouraged the EPA from interfering. George Bush's labor secretary was Elaine Chao, wife of Kentucky's Mitch McConnell, U.S. Senate minor-ity leader and the most abject coal whore outside the state of West Virginia. Bonds never expected much from politicians. "In Appa-lachia, I think ninety-eight percent of the politicians are corrupt," she said. "They owe their souls to coal."

For defenders of the mountains, it's always been a hard uphill climb. Not content with owning local judges and officials, Blan-kenship, a Far-Right Republican in a Democratic state, opened his checkbook to the Tea Party movement. What's not to like, he reasoned, about poor and lower-middle-class Americans who *vol-unteer* to defend the rights of the rich and the profits of big cor-porations? Flanked by TV demagogues like Sean Hannity, the Dark Lord seemed as comfortable haranguing Tea Parties as in-timidating miners. The feisty, plain-spoken Bonds, who became a

compelling speaker on the environmental circuit, addressed much
smaller but much smarter audiences. She had some encouraging
moments, most notably when she won the prestigious Goldman
Environmental Prize, with its $150,000 stipend, in 2003. But the
national media paid little attention to a crisis in Appalachia, she
said, and she predicted, "It's going to take blood before anyone
will notice."

Her oracular pronouncement proved prophetic. The election of
Barack Obama meant a more alert and sympathetic EPA, but it
took blood and disaster to tip the scales. In April 2010, a buildup
of coal dust and methane exploded in Massey's much-cited Up-
per Big Branch mine, killing twenty-nine miners. It was the worst
loss of life in the coalfields in forty years, and the beginning of
the end for Don Blankenship. His remorse was typically inadequate, and when company records showed that he had specifically ordered supervisors to place production before safety, many
of Massey's shareholders began to squirm. The final straw was a
profile of Blankenship in *Rolling Stone*, titled "The Dark Lord of
Coal Country," that left few gaps in the chilling biography of a
native Appalachian monster. (For a fuller portrait of Judy Bonds,
read her chapter in *Something's Rising*, a tribute to Appalachia's
Green heroes written by Silas House and Jason Howard and published by the University of Kentucky Press.)

Of course Judy Bonds was fighting cancer, an even tougher ad-
versary, as Blankenship's empire was crumbling. And of course
she had no illusions that his successor would be gentle and Green,
or that the EPA would revoke the rest of its mountaintop removal
permits. As her health declined, Don Blankenship was probably

lounging on his yacht in the Caribbean instead of drowning in a poison slurry pond or suffocating in a collapsing mineshaft as he no doubt deserved. But hope was in the air, competing with the coal dust. And in West Virginia, where fear is a legacy and black lung a family tradition, a little hope goes a long, long way.

Bonds and Blankenship didn't move in the same circles in West Virginia, and there's no chance at all that they'll meet in the Hereafter. Yet saying a proper farewell to Judy Bonds means recognizing that this epic confrontation between a working-class hero of conscience and a genuine nineteenth-century robber baron is emblematic of a struggle at the core of the American experience. Citizens like Judy Bonds are what this country has to produce if it hopes to survive; citizens like Don Blankenship are what it has to eliminate. The Blankenship quotation that should go on his tombstone is this one: "I don't care what people think. At the end of the day, Don Blankenship is going to die with more money than he needs." There's a relevant response among one of the many wise and striking things Bonds will be remembered for saying. "My grandson told me he had picked out an escape route in case the dam [for coal waste] failed," she recalled. "I knew in my heart there was really no escape. How do you tell a child that his life is a sacrifice for corporate greed?"

Note: In May 2018 the felon Blankenship, who served a year in prison, ran unsuccessfully for a U.S. Senate seat in the 2018 West Virginia Republican primary.

FRANK M. JOHNSON

The Last Southern Hero

MAYBE IT'S A deliberate provocation to style Frank M. Johnson, Jr., "the last Southern hero." It invites conflict with people who hold to different definitions of *hero*, others who hold to rigid definitions of *Southern*. But I have a strong case to argue, and Judge Johnson, on his part, never shrank from conflict when the case before him was a strong one.

Martin Luther King, Jr., called him "a man who gave true meaning to the word 'justice.'" For Southern liberals and veterans of the civil rights movement, Johnson has been a gigantic figure since the '50s, when his landmark rulings as a federal judge for the Middle

District of Alabama established him as Jim Crow's most powerful natural enemy.

"The most influential, innovative, controversial trial judge in the United States," Alabama Senator Howell Heflin called Johnson. *Time* magazine, in a 1967 cover story, hailed him as "one of the most important men in America." To Robert F. Kennedy, Jr., one of Johnson's biographers, "he's as much an American hero as the leaders of the Revolutionary War and the Civil War."

"If he had been born one hundred years earlier he would have been Abraham Lincoln, or vice versa," Bill Moyers enthused after his interview with Johnson.

America has experienced some sea changes since the high tide of Frank Johnson's influence. Judicial activism, which he personified, is in darkest disfavor with a conservative Supreme Court. Affirmative action, which in many jurists' eyes was Johnson's personal invention, is rejected by a majority and detested as the devil's worst work by the judge's own Republican Party. The party of Lincoln to which he was devoted has become the party of Jesse Helms, David Duke, and the whole rabble of Dixiecrat racialists he labored to frustrate and defeat.

These sea changes haven't eroded Johnson's legacy, which has been written into law and legal precedent that a century of political reaction won't eradicate. But they've reduced public consciousness of his achievements, chipped away at his myth. It's as if a nation of backsliders, ashamed to look its judicial conscience square in the eye—Johnson's laser blue eyes that drove weak lawyers to wet themselves—had left his portrait hanging but turned it to the wall.

When Johnson died in the summer of 1999, at eighty, America

was too wrapped up in the death of John F. Kennedy, Jr., to pay much attention. Judge Johnson outlived, by nearly a year, his life-long nemesis George Wallace, whose death in 1998 was similarly obscured by the tabloid abomination historians will be forced to call the Lewinsky Impeachment. In a thirty-year morality play with the soul of the South in the balance, Frank Johnson played the white knight and George Wallace wore black, and the issue that was decided between these onetime friends and law school class-mates was arguably the most important issue America resolved in our lifetime. Their duel made compelling history and classic drama, but by the time these epic antagonists took their final cur-tain call, everyone had left the theater.

"Timing is everything," Johnson might have said, with laconic humility. He could use that for an epitaph. It was perfect timing—for a lone Eisenhower Republican in all-Democratic Alabama—that made him a U.S. Attorney at thirty-four and a federal judge at thirty-seven, the youngest one in the country. It was perfect tim-ing, for the segregated and intimidated black people of Alabama, that placed Johnson on the court in 1955, just in time to teach George Wallace that the Supreme Court was serious about *Brown v. Board of Education.* A self-styled hillbilly from Northern Ala-bama, Johnson arrived in Montgomery with no debts or ties to the Democratic establishment, and when the civil rights wars came to Alabama, his singularity made all the difference.

It was poor timing, on the other hand, when surgery on a near-fatal aneurysm in 1977 forced him to resign his nomination as di-rector of the FBI. And poor timing again when Jimmy Carter's defeat in 1980, along with the right-wing takeover of the Republican Party, left him without a friend in the White House at a time when he was clearly the leading candidate for the next vacancy on the U.S. Supreme Court. It was tragic poor timing, in 1975, when Johnson arrived a minute too late to prevent his son Johnny, his only child, from locking himself in their house and committing suicide with a shotgun.

Frank Johnson was the last Southern hero because we're suffering a general extinction of heroes, along with the apparent extinction of the individual and the meaningful community (it was reported that millions mourned JKF, Jr., in Internet chat rooms—a glutinous mass of media slaves mourning a man they never met with people they've never seen). But ultimately he's our last hero because we've come to the end of the time when the South's problems are unique to the South.

Timing is everything, for heroes. In drab times, heroes-who-might-have-been file by untested, unsuspected, unfulfilled. In an age of computers, Hercules would be a terrorist or a professional wrestler. Frank Johnson was lucky, if that's the right word, to have walked onstage at a moment in history when a great judge could play a critical role.

Biographers have made much of the fact that Johnson was born and raised in rural Winston County, an enclave of hardcase North Alabama hill farmers who owned few slaves and objected so strenuously to secession that they assembled at Looney's Tavern in 1862, 2,500 strong, and declared their intention to secede from the state of Alabama. "The Free State of Winston" never saw the light of day, but most Winston men enlisted in the Union Army, more than twice as many as the Confederacy recruited. Two volunteers for the First Alabama Cavalry Regiment of the United States Army were Reuben and Moses Johnson, Frank Johnson's great-great-uncles, who came home from the war to find that rebel sympathizers had stolen all their horses and cattle (they reclaimed them at gunpoint).

Johnson's family tree is crawling with ferocious independents, lone wolves, and outright contrarians. His maternal great-grandfather, Francis Marion Treadaway, fought for the Confederacy but distinguished himself as a sheriff who routed the Ku Klux Klan; his father, Frank Johnson, Sr., was once the only Republican in the Alabama legislature. But the virtues and attitudes that set Frank Johnson apart are ones many small-town, up-country Americans can find in themselves.

Johnson's biographer Jack Bass (*Taming the Storm: The Life and Times of Judge Frank M. Johnson, Jr.*, 1993) refers to the "classless" tradition of rural places with no local aristocracy. If you grew up respectable in a town like Double Springs, AL, you acknowledged no one above you. In the interview with Bill Moyers, Johnson summed up the small-town point of view: "People in that section of the country have a fiercely independent attitude and personality. They have an intense respect for the individual and the individual's right. They believe in a person's dignity, and they believe each person is possessed of and is entitled to integrity. They believe that without regard to race, creed, color, or ideology. 'Every man's his own man' is a real basic philosophy."

Johnson is usually described as fearless, but *stubborn* was the word his friends used. Neither the stick nor the carrot will move the kind of mule they breed in Winston County. Segregationists

never understood how much their cause was damaged when racist thugs burned a cross on Johnson's lawn, and firebombed his
mother's house; Montgomery society never understood how little
he cared for country club memberships or invitations to black-
tie balls. Judge Johnson's recollection of one such occasion is a
cracker-barrel classic: "Went to one. These men sixty-five or seventy years old with white gloves and all that sort of stuff. Some of
them with monkey suits on. Doing a lot of drinking. Late in the
evening challenging each other to a duel. Ruth said I talked too
loud. Biggest bunch of bullshit I've ever seen."

His lone-wolf Winston ways—deploring injustice but doubting
the government's ability to set it right—often placed Johnson at
odds with the consensus-building, bureaucracy-trusting Northern
Democrats who came to save Alabama in the '60s. Frank Johnson
was not your man to join hands and sing the anthems of Odetta
and Joan Baez.

His decisions desegregating Alabama's schools, buses, and voting booths (and humanizing its prisons and mental institutions)
were never motivated by a liberal, bleeding-heart ideology—only
by what he perceived to be fair, reasonable, legal, and part of his
jurisdiction. He outraged civil rights activists with some of his
rulings and once threatened to "put some Klansmen, some po-
licemen, and some Negro preachers" in Atlanta Penitentiary side
by side.

He'd have been wounded if he thought most of his mourn-
ers would be Yankees. A tobacco-chewing, bass-fishing, George
Dickel–drinking country lawyer, Frank Johnson was Alabama to
the bone. Hell, his mother was named Alabama—Alabama Long.

Of all the abuse Johnson suffered, none was more unjust than the yellow-journalists' assertion that he was an unnatural native son, an alien creature of Northern institutions and Northern conspiracies. "Carpetbagger" was the least of the epithets visited on Judge Johnson by George Wallace, who once suggested that he could benefit from "a barbed-wire enema."

"You work for Frank Johnson?" a Montgomery butcher asked one of Johnson's law clerks. "When he dies, people are going to line up to piss on his grave"—a queue that never materialized.

Dixie's diehards are glacially slow to forgive Southerners who stood up for different principles, in 1860 or 1960, and saw those principles prevail. It will be a cold August in Birmingham when most Alabamans concede that Frank Johnson's ancestors were right about secession. Officially, they've already conceded that Johnson was right about segregation. In 1992 the federal courthouse in Montgomery was renamed in the judge's honor, and a bronze bust of Johnson was placed in the lobby.

It was more reconciliation than Frank Johnson expected or required. When George Wallace called to ask the Johnsons to forgive him, he was rebuffed. The judge had reached a decision that he refused to reverse on appeal, even for an old man in a wheelchair: "George sent me a message that he wanted forgiveness. I sent him a message back that if he wanted to get forgiveness, he'd have to get it from the Lord."

JESSE HELMS

The Last of His Kind?

JESSE HELMS DIED on the Fourth of July, 2008, a coincidence that certain patriots noted with pride. Newspaper obituaries were surprisingly kind. They dutifully noted that the ex-senator gave good constituent service, adopted a handicapped child, raised money for worthy charities, made time to talk to high school students. That's as it should be, I guess. When I die, I hope someone will mention that I loved dogs, never beat my children, and was unfailingly courteous to older women. But another North Carolina public servant, L. F. Eason III, became one of my citizen idols when he defied the governor's directive to fly state flags at half-staff in memory of Sen. Helms. Eason, manager of the state meteorology laboratory, resigned from the only job he'd ever held rather than lower the flags at his building to honor Helms. Leaving the Agricultural Department after twenty-nine years of service, Eason cited Helms's "doctrine of negativity, hate and prejudice."

To put it mildly. Jesse, mercifully the last of his kind, was a one-man roadblock on North Carolina's path to self-respect. Every few years the political universe would shift a few degrees to the right and the national media would rediscover Jesse Helms. Astonishment was followed by angry editorials and wild stabs at psycho-biography. My God, he's still there, they'd announce. Bleeding-heart New Yorkers would volunteer for Peace Corps assignments in darkest Charlotte. A Manhattan hostess would ask me where I was from and then ask me how I ever found the stomach to stay.

Rediscovering Jesse was like rediscovering the La Brea tar pits. These are ugly, ancient things that don't go away. But unlike Los Angeles, which built a modern city around its tar pits, North Carolina made no effort to conceal or improve upon the sticky black hole of Jesse's ignorance, where the fossilized remains of his Cenozoic ancestors lay entombed. If anything, we treated him like a tourist attraction.

We appreciated the nation's sympathy. We deserved it. But it's not as if Jesse Helms floated up in front of the sun every morning like the Goodyear blimp and cast a fist-shaped shadow from Murphy to Manteo; the air temperature would drop a few degrees, birds would cease their song, blue-tick hounds would howl mournfully, and liberals slink off to their secular prayers behind locked doors.

It wasn't like that at all. The chorus of amazement that accompanied each rediscovery actually tickled most of us. We got to be experts again and take calls from out-of-state reporters who were in high school the last time Jesse was discovered. I had my fun. For a while I wore a Jesse Helms watch someone gave me. It told time in reverse, of course, counterclockwise. Once I called Helms "a mascot, a huge old pit bull, useless and vicious, that sits in its own mess at the end of a tow-truck chain and snarls at everything that moves."

I received the great compliment of seeing that image stolen without apology by the *New York Times*, which probably thinks no one writing down here reads the *Times* or understands copyright. Another time I compared Jesse to Grendel, but his brain trust at the Congressional Club probably told him I meant Fred Grendle, who runs the feed store up on Rte. 158 between Oxford and Berea.

Jesse was such a wonderful foil and such a gifted comedian in his own right, it's a good thing humorless liberals would break in from time to time to remind us that life with Jesse wasn't all songs and skits.

If Jesse and the segregationists hadn't bushwhacked Sen. Frank Porter Graham in 1950, North Carolina might have become a state everyone could be proud of, with real pride instead of the Chamber of Commerce variety. Instead of a backsliding contradiction of a state where pockets of progress and talent are surrounded by a wilderness of reaction and racial resentment, and where nearly a million people live below the poverty line.

Nelson Mandela might have been out of prison ten years earlier, if Helms and other racists hadn't sent South Africa the quasi-official message that a lot of Americans thought Mandela was right where he belonged. Jesse was the one who would have needed bodyguards if he ever visited El Salvador or Nicaragua (or Fire Island).

There are checkpoints on the highway to heaven where the angels will take a hard look at that thing old Jesse calls his soul. But what he was selling, in his awful prime, was mainly nostalgia. Nostalgia for the good old days when a Coke cost a nickel, everybody was a Baptist who talked like Sam Ervin, and weird sex was anything you did with the lights on. When you could sit on your porch and talk to someone across the street, with no traffic to drown out your voices.

Most of us from small towns feel this same sense of loss and displacement. Unfortunately, Jesse's customers were all white people, and in North Carolina white nostalgia for the good old days usually includes nostalgia for separate restrooms and lunch counters.

A vote for Jesse Helms was a vote for their ancestors. At one time North Carolina was begging for the Disney Corporation's historical theme park. But our senator was a walking theme park with two themes, Jim Crow and the Cold War.

They were the pole stars of his life. In each case containment was the thing. A man could get a good night's sleep if he knew the colored and the communists were in their proper places, on the other side of the tracks and the other side of the world. But it took a viable threat to keep them in their place.

This world that produced Jesse Helms seems prehistoric here in the twenty-first century. Did the last prominent relic of the old Jim Crow/John Birch South ever pose a viable threat to the security of America? I didn't think so. Aside from his refreshing sense of humor (who else could have added "garden-variety lesbian" to the Senate lexicon?), there's no compelling evidence to refute the theory that Jesse was a moron. Think of Forrest Gump's cranky older brother, with a toothache.

In the flexible profession of politics, he was the rarest thing of all, a flatliner—a man who practiced politics for fifty years with no discernible learning curve. No one accused Jesse Helms of being a satanic hypocrite. He mastered a kind of hit-and-run style, wisecracking out of closing elevators and car windows. But when you trapped him in front of a microphone, he was a tongue-tied, slightly bewildered old guy who sounded about as cerebral as most of his true believers.

Making Jesse chairman of the Senate Foreign Relations Committee was a piece of comic inspiration, like naming Barney Fife to direct the FBI. Who said Republicans have no sense of humor? Who said history has no sense of humor?

If someone like Ollie North had been elected president, of course, he and Jesse and a Republican Congress might have unraveled forty years of skilled diplomacy in six months. But even as chairman, Helms offered little more than his usual noise and nuisance. In a period of national realignment and right-wing evangelism, Jesse Helms might have been the best thing poor liberals and moderates had left in their arsenal. His national approval rating, around 13 percent, was one-third of Bill Clinton's worst ever. The country could never have gone all the way back to Jesse. Too many young people, immigrants, and nonwhites could never imagine the small-town Southern world that created him. He served the nation as a kind of navigational marker, a fixed thing to steer away from if you hoped to keep yourself from grounding on dangerous shoals. The whole political spectrum has shifted to the Right dramatically, but as long as Jesse lived we could always find Too Far.

If only all the reactionaries were like Jesse Helms, painted purple with a big necklace fashioned from the jawbones of civil-rights workers and Latin American peasants. If only they were all Macy's Parade–size and trailing long kite-tails of errors, absurdities, and unbelievable quotes on everything from art to apartheid.

It's the camouflaged ones, the ones who seem to look alike and think alike, the Christianized consumers with identical Lite-Right lives who scare the daylights out of me. Who can tell them from ordinary citizens until some door slams shut and they've got us? Jesse was so much easier. You could see him coming from a hundred miles away.

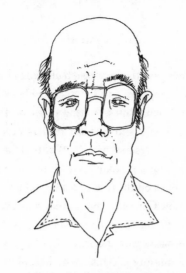

WILL CAMPBELL

God's Will

ACK IN THE early '90s, my wife and I were in Nashville for the Southern Festival of Books, one of the first I attended, and I was impressed to see that a generous number of black writers had been invited to read and present their books. But I had time to circulate and noticed an uncomfortable fact of book life. (It's my curse to notice uncomfortable facts where others see only serendipity.) In the lines where purchasing readers waited to get the writers' signatures on their books—Jimmy Carter's line was two blocks long, I remember—it was painfully obvious that black readers were buying from black writers, and white readers from whites.

Book-signing lines gave the impression of being segregated. There was one flagrant exception, a fully integrated book line, with perhaps more blacks than whites, waiting to secure the signature of the Rev. Will Campbell. And his black readers were not customers only, but apparently personal friends. Way back in the line people were hollering at him and joking with him, so much that it was hard for him to focus on the title pages he was trying to sign.

I hadn't met Rev. Campbell, nor at that time even read his celebrated memoir, *Brother to a Dragonfly*. I knew him by reputation only, an alternative sort of clergyman who served as unofficial chaplain to a community of Music City irregulars. As a spiritual advisor he came highly recommended by a wide range of Nashville types that included some of our friends. I'd heard that his chaplaincy at the University of Mississippi, in his native state, had been terminated because his enthusiasm for integration attracted death threats. I'd heard that he drank beer with Thomas Merton. I didn't realize the extent of his involvement in the civil rights movement of the '60s. I was not aware that he was the only white man invited to the meeting that launched the Southern Christian Leadership Conference, that he had marched with Freedom Riders in Alabama and run the gauntlet of racist thugs with the nine black students who integrated Central High School in Little Rock. For those who knew that he was a trusted friend and confidant of Martin Luther King, Jr., the lone white friend who came to pray with King's family after the assassination in Memphis, I guess it was no surprise to see black people hailing him like family in Nashville.

Later I had the good fortune to join Campbell's extended congregation, a privilege that included pilgrimages to his home place in Mt. Juliet, TN, where pastoral consultations might include drinking whiskey and listening to Will sing scabrous ballads, to his own guitar accompaniment. Cussing and praying were not incompatible in his religious worldview, where the sacred and the profane were as inseparable as God's children, white and black and all shades in between. In Mt. Juliet no pilgrims were turned away, and none were confronted with their sins and errors. Will could homilize with the best of them, but he was just as comfortable listening, nodding benevolently, whittling away at the whimsical walking sticks he bestowed on his friends. Nonjudgmental? That's not for me to say. Rev. Campbell was nonjudgmental *on the surface*, to a fault. Like many people who influence others profoundly, he combined ample external confidence with a core of impregnable humility.

It's unnecessary to explain, to anyone who knew Will Campbell, why he was one of the most remarkable and valuable Southerners of his generation. Mention his name and his parishioners will just grin and shake their heads. But for those who never had the privilege of meeting him, it's important to place him in a proper context, free of stereotypes and received ideas. He was invariably described as a "maverick," "renegade," or "curmudgeon," words that subtly, sometimes condescendingly, distance their subject from the mainstream of respectable opinion. Just a shade removed from "crank," "curmudgeon" is often fastened to citizens who bear truths that not everyone wishes to hear. Campbell bore many in his time. But he was never a calculating contrarian, ever a by-God original. He believed in the Gospel of Jesus Christ, put it on like a coat that fit him and took it places where it hadn't gone before. Of the many categories that included him—Christian, Southern Baptist, clergyman, theologian, liberal (even "redneck," which he embraced cheerfully as long as it came without a Yankee sneer)—there was not one of which Will Campbell was even remotely typical.

"I'm seventy-six, I've been all over the world, and I've only met one Will Campbell," marvels Nashville songwriter Tom T. Hall, a longtime admirer. "There must be something special about him." What set him way apart, to begin with, was a moral compass tuned to True North—or True South, I suppose. A south-Mississippi "deep water" Baptist who was called to preach the Gospel at the age of seventeen, he derived his politics and theology from the New Testament as he interpreted it—not from his intellectual friends, though he had plenty, or from other books, though he'd read plenty, too. The Sermon on the Mount was the text for his belief that a true Christian always sides with the powerless and the marginalized. The chasm of difference between Will Campbell and those Southern preachers better known to America—Jerry Falwell, Pat Robertson, Jim Bakker, Jimmy Swaggart, even the sincere but intellectually challenged Billy Graham—is so vast that only Jesus could have bridged it. Will once described televangelists as "electronic soul molesters" and admitted that they sorely tested his personal gospel of unconditional forgiveness.

In one sense Jesus is always an imagined figure, historically indistinct and far away, and the great strength of rare believers like Will is that they can imagine Christ so vividly they almost resurrect him, body and blood. It's likely that the actual Jesus would have abhorred many Southern Christians, for their hypocrisy and false piety and especially for their preposterous certainty—always denied, yet pathetically obvious—that Heaven itself was segregated. And perhaps Hell as well. But Jesus, despite language barriers and culture gaps, would surely have taken a shine to Will Campbell. When I compare Brother Will to some oleaginous bigot like Pat Robertson, I think of the scene in *Crocodile Dundee* when a New York thug pulls a knife on Paul Hogan and Hogan, producing a blade the size of a scimitar, says "That's not a knife—*this* is a knife!" That's not a Christian—*this* is a Christian!

A lesson all Will's congregants learned well is the difference between a commitment to social justice, which means acting always in a way that you believe will help the underdog to prevail, and political correctness, which means always agreeing with the underdog and parroting his language on every issue that concerns him. Rev. Campbell, who chewed tobacco and deplored abortion, was about as PC as a Bengal tiger, and he valued knee-jerk liberals about as highly as televangelists. The night before Will's memorial service, I had dinner with North Carolina novelist Wayne Caldwell, another Campbellite, who complained that New Yorkers have asked him how he could call himself a Baptist, as if that was synonymous with superstition and political reaction. "I tell them I'm a Will Campbell Baptist," Caldwell said, "and let them figure it out."

He wrote a dozen books and won prizes for many of them, but not every chapter and verse of the Gospel According to Will was crystal clear to his adherents, not even to the most loyal and attentive. The writer John Egerton, who was Will's close friend for decades and in later years served him as a kind of consigliere, admitted after Campbell's death that the holy man's logic sometimes escaped him. "I never understood a lot about him," Egerton allowed. "But he was no phony." Particularly difficult for Christians of weaker conviction was Will's insistence that Jesus forgave the worst criminals while their hands were still bloody, a radical belief that compelled him to counsel Klansmen and racist assassins and to visit James Earl Ray, King's murderer, in his prison cell. "Hate the sin, not the sinner," is an ambitious moral goal to which many pay lip service (most often, it seems, to deny their homophobia), but Will Campbell made it the cornerstone of his faith. As he was quoted repeatedly, "If you're gonna love one, you've got to love 'em all."

The way Campbell saw it, only a small percentage of God's children can ever find and steer their lives by the light of reason, but that didn't exclude the rest of His children from the light of His love. Who, Will might ask, needs help—or love—more than a benighted, hate-poisoned Klansman? I could see the sense in that. But the old deep-water religion and the doctrine of universal amnesty were a harder sell to someone like me, the product on the one hand of four generations of Unitarians and, on the other, of untold centuries of vengeful Celts. But Will didn't proselytize; he was a pastor, a shepherd, not an evangelist. If you disagreed with him, he only needed to be sure that you'd thought it through with care, that you hadn't recycled some cheap piece of conventional wisdom. If you said something harsh or stupid in his presence, he'd look at you with mild disappointment, as if he'd just bitten into a sour apple, and with real concern, as if he was ready to help you if you asked him. Such was the agreeable flavor of his ministry.

It was a hard road Campbell set himself to travel, and he could be hard on himself. He warned me once about a bad person we both knew—I wish I had listened more carefully—but what tormented Will was not the trespass committed against him but his uphill struggle to forgive the trespasser unconditionally. A friend described Will as "obsessed with grace." He was one of a kind, a Dixie Diogenes navigating by his own light, searching for honesty and virtue in a troubled land. This was a Depression-era cotton farmer's son from Jim Crow Mississippi who decided, at the age of twenty, "This is what I will do with the rest of my life—try to rectify the evils of racial injustice." His underdog theology led him from integration to the antiwar movement, to denouncing capital punishment and championing the rights of women and gay people. At a time when the South as a whole is not distinguishing itself for creative thinking, moral vision, or progressive politics, we might ask ourselves how someone like Will Campbell came about. Could we clone him, find a way to breed more of him, or was he just a rare gift from a tired gene pool—or as he might say (but never about himself), a manifestation of the grace of God?

"Will Campbell was a sage," eulogized Congressman John Lewis, a surviving hero of the civil rights movement. "He was a gift to America who never received the recognition he truly deserved." Another admirer characterized Will as "a man of many disguises," and as John Lewis and his colleagues remember him, he sounds almost like the Lone Ranger—wherever injustice and oppression soiled the Southland he would appear mysteriously, a black hat on his head and forgiveness in his heart. The day he was memorialized in Nashville, my wife and I held our own modest memorial in the Yankee-haunted north woods, a service which consisted mostly of listening to gospel standards recorded by the late great sinner George Jones, Nashville's second most painful loss in the spring of 2013. "It Is No Secret" was the one that choked me up: "With arms wide open, He'll pardon you . . ." ("It is no secret what God can do.") Right, Will. Sometimes—this time, anyway—I think I get it.

GEORGE WALLACE

Requiem for a Bantamweight

T HE LITTLE BULLDOG has made his last headlines, and they were inadequate. Coinciding exactly with the loathsome climax to the most bizarre, corrosive sex scandal in American history, the death of George Wallace was almost overlooked by the overheated media machinery. Coked up on legal pornography, free at last from the burdens of memory or responsibility, the national media barely looked up from their keyholes to acknowledge the death of a sick old man in a wheelchair, a politician whose last run for office was in 1982. In the hysteria of yet another tabloid stampede, few hands were available to accord this singular life the editorial consideration it deserved. A year ago the same thing happened to Mother Teresa, an irony Governor Wallace would have appreciated.

You were cheated, George. I remember when they wouldn't leave you alone. But you died in a state of dignity, you SOB, holding your head higher than most of your newsroom enemies, those city Yankees who treated you like the slimiest thing to crawl out of Dixie since Simon Legree.

Journalist Teddy White, who made a career of presidential politics, dismissed George Wallace as "a narrow-minded, grossly provincial man" and "a Southern populist of the meanest streak."

But where, now, is the liberal press that installed Teddy White as a guru—and where is the presidency?

Only the historians are left to judge George Wallace now. They'll rank him—serious historians have already ranked him—as one of the most influential political figures of the twentieth century. As a fledgling moderate in a state dominated by white racists, young Wallace took his first electoral licking and swore his famous oath that he'd never be "out-niggered" by another political opponent.

"I started out talking about schools and highways and prisons and taxes, and I couldn't make them listen," he once confessed ruefully to an Alabama newspaper editor. "Then I began talking about niggers—and they stomped the floor."

Wallace fashioned himself into a fire-breathing segregationist who came to own the state of Alabama as completely as Huey Long once owned Louisiana. His favorite speechwriter, author of Wallace's defiant "Segregation now . . . segregation tomorrow . . . segregation forever!" was Asa "Ace" Carter, a ferocious Klan terrorist linked to the 1956 castration of a retarded black handyman, a victim chosen at random as a warning to "troublemakers." (In one of history's more improbable footnotes, Ace Carter fled to Texas and shed his Alabama identity like a snakeskin. He became Forrest Carter, the "Native American" author of a best-selling novel, *The Education of Little Tree*, the high-minded story of a young Cherokee's coming-of-age.)

Those were ugly times in Alabama, and George Wallace made himself as ugly as his tireless ambition required. The divisive politics he perfected were nothing new in his part of the South. But Wallace preached his white supremacy with a soulful blend of heartfelt populism, a little man's fierce determination to fight the system that sold him short.

It was a blend that mobilized resentful underdogs wherever he took his message. If the pitch was tailored to suit his audience, there was nothing calculating about the pit-bull pugnacity Wallace radiated. As a pint-sized teenager he was one of the most celebrated boxers in the South, twice bantamweight Golden Gloves champion of Alabama, runner-up in the 1936 Southern finals in Nashville. An indomitable counterpuncher, Wallace was defeated just four times in his life. That belligerent thrust of his jaw, interpreted by gentler souls as pure redneck meanness, said to Americans with hard lives and losing records that he was a champion who could take a punch and never quit on them.

Wallace came as close as any overtly racist politician to converting America to the wisdom of Old Alabama. As a third-party candidate for president, he was primarily responsible for the Waterloo of American liberalism, the narrow defeat of Hubert Humphrey in

1968. In 1972, Wallace dominated the Democratic primaries until he was shot in Maryland in May. According to historian Dan T. Carter (in his Wallace biography, *The Politics of Rage*), these Wallace campaigns inspired Richard Nixon—at the urging of speechwriter Pat Buchanan—to adopt his successful "Southern strategy" of 1972.

In direct consequence, Carter argues, reactionaries seized the Republican Party, American electoral politics underwent permanent realignment, and an unlikely alliance between Wall Street and Tobacco Road elected Ronald Reagan. ("Wall Street—," wrote Lillian Smith, "that fabulous crooked canyon of evil winding endlessly through the Southern mind.")

This unnatural alliance is the most dominant force—some would say the most toxic force—in national politics today. Dan Carter says we owe it all to George Wallace. A yellow-dog Democrat who grew up worshipping Franklin Delano Roosevelt, Wallace was the model and catalyst for a right-wing revolution that swept away nearly everything the New Deal espoused or achieved. But in farewell we should note that the governor was always true, in his fashion, to his beloved FDR. He was ever the populist who took his guidance from the man in the street.

It was the Republican Party and its surviving racialist demagogues, like Jesse Helms, who devised the post-populist Raw Deal— a corporate fast shuffle that promises poor whites nothing whatsoever except a worse deal for black people. And it still works, as George Wallace could have predicted from his first political lesson in Alabama long ago.

Wallace watched most of this from a wheelchair. Crippled by

an assassin's bullets at the height of his influence—he'd just won a primary in Michigan and finished second in Pennsylvania and Indiana—he recovered enough to make a die-hard last run at the presidency in 1976. He never relinquished his grip on Alabama, not until age and chronic pain took the edge off his lifelong hunger to rule the roost.

In his suffering, dreadful by all accounts, Wallace converted to a new vision of racial harmony. He disavowed the politics of rage and made public acts of contrition to black leaders like Jesse Jackson. There were those who remained skeptical about the sincerity of Wallace's conversion. Dan Carter quotes a Wallace aide, John Kohn, who said, "Hell, George could believe whatever he needed to believe." But the black voters of Alabama believed him, enough to give him 90 percent of their votes the last time he was elected governor, in 1982.

He had a hell of a life when you think about it, a life with drama, sweep, tragedy, agony, redemption. It was a big life, a big role for a little man, a farmer's son (but a doctor's grandson) from Clio, Alabama. The cast of characters was fascinating, with friends and enemies of equal luster. John F. Kennedy detested Wallace and refused to be photographed with him; a hidden photographer with a telephoto lens captured their one recorded handshake, as JFK disembarked from an Army helicopter on his Alabama visit of May 1963. Elvis Presley loved George Wallace and often sought his advice. Elvis once swore he'd personally kill Arthur Bremer, the gunman who paralyzed Wallace in 1972.

The bantamweight from Clio has thrown his last punch. Under normal circumstances this would be an occasion for stock-taking, a time when the South might find some satisfaction in a moral inventory. The most vivid symbol of its ancestral transgressions is gone—and he departed repentant, shriven and forgiven and ready for whatever grace the next place allows.

In states where juries routinely acquitted unrepentant Klan killers, a new generation of jurors and prosecutors has snatched some of the old dragons from their cozy retirement and sent them where they belong. In 1994 a Mississippi jury convicted Medgar Evers's murderer, Bryon De La Beckwith. In Hattiesburg, Mississippi, a jury of six blacks, five whites, and an Asian found onetime Imperial Wizard Samuel Bowers, seventy-three, guilty of the firebombing murder of Vernon Dahmer, Sr., in 1966. In South Carolina, a jury assessed punitive damages of $38 million against Klansmen who burned a black church in 1955.

The voice—the voice of the killer Klansman that Eudora Welty reproduced so chillingly in her story "Where Is the Voice Coming From?"—isn't much more than a whisper now. The South still leads the nation in murder, by a wide margin, but the murder rate has fallen 25 percent since 1978, and in most cases blacks and whites murder their own. A black historian from my own Carolina neighborhood, John Hope Franklin, chaired the president's elite panel on racial relations in America. Politically correct critics who deny that we've seen any racial progress are as irritating as the fools who say everything is fine.

Journalist John Egerton once said that it would be "a wonderful irony" if Southerners were the ones to lead the rest of the nation toward a resolution of our economic and racial inequalities. Isn't it pretty to think so? But I see a more somber irony. By the time the Old Confederacy has made full amends for its sins—all the amends it can make at this point, or could be expected to make—the Republic it rejoined in 1865 will be so far gone to other false gods and fierce creeds, there'll be no one around to accept our credentials and declare us healed. I don't know how you feel about Washington, about the people who make the news there, or the people who report it. But if those are the people who set the moral bar Southerners are supposed to vault over, it might be high time to consider a second Act of Secession. It's a response George Wallace, always Washington's nemesis and nightmare, would understand as well as Jefferson Davis.

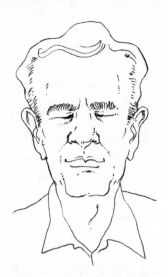

DOC WATSON

But Now I See

I have seen the David, I've seen the Mona Lisa too
And I have heard Doc Watson play Columbus Stockade Blues.
—Guy Clark, "Dublin Blues"

THE MERLE WATSON Festival is a four-day celebration that stops only to sleep, and not for long either. By day four, a Sunday, even younger people try to pace themselves. But one promising Sunday morning four or five years ago, we committed ourselves to a sunrise gospel session, which meant coffee in the dark and a long drive down the mountain in the fog. Our commitment was rewarded, beyond all mortal expectations, by a once-in-a-lifetime gospel trio of Doc Watson, Ralph Stanley, and Emmylou Harris.

We came in on "Heaven's Bright Shore," followed by "Rank Stranger" and "I'll Pass Over Thee." For an hour or so, forty lucky pilgrims shared a privileged preview of Hillbilly Heaven. I feel sorry for ticketholders who actually went to church that Sunday morning. I'm afraid they were cheated, because there in the corner of the gospel tent—singing along in a soft clear bass—was a big old mountaineer with a salt-and-pepper ponytail who looked an awful lot like God.

The trio wound up their set with "Amazing Grace." Harris wore her church face and sang the high notes like a bourbon-frosted angel. Stanley stood ramrod straight like he does, like he's standing to hear his sentence in the court of Final Judgment. When they reached "I once was blind, but now I see," I took a hard look at Doc Watson to see if I could pick up anything wistful or ironic on his face.

Doc just looked comfortable and spiritual, the same as he looked when he played at my college in 1963, in the heat of the great folk revival. New England had never seen anything like Doc. For weeks after, preppies from Connecticut with expensive Martin guitars were trying to lower their voices and flat-pick their own way through "Tennessee Stud." A year earlier, half of them had been listening to Fabian.

I was stunned by Doc's performance, and suspected for the first time that those mountains, which I'd been trying to escape all my life, might be harboring things I ought to be proud of. In those days it was still possible, I think, for an unsophisticated person to be ambushed by sheer authenticity, to be knocked flat and left in the road by something undeniably real.

I never imagined that he'd be my neighbor someday, that I'd buy a house just two ridges over from the Watson homeplace and get to hear Doc play for free at his cousin's twelve-table fish restaurant on the road to Boone, NC, under a sign that says "Friends Gather Here."

I suppose I saw him perform a hundred times. Most worthwhile people knew that Doc Watson was a blind guitarist, blind not quite from birth but from infancy. Over the years Doc almost convinced me that blindness is no obstacle for a born musician.

"Music is sound," Watson told one interviewer. "You learn where the notes are because of the sound of them. You don't have to see to play the guitar."

From watching Doc, I'll even argue that there's a different quality to a blind musician's performance, often a superior quality. When he makes the connection with his audience, it's all-consuming. He's so much with them because it's his one moment, his chance—because when the connection is broken he's so much alone.

Backstage, Doc would sit immobile, supernaturally patient, with what I interpreted as exquisitely tuned attention. I believed he could hear a string break or a note misplayed three tents away, over the roar of the multitude. The ears of blind musicians are the finest instruments they own. Ray Charles once heard the Rolling Stones live and declared their decibel level unbearable. "I thought I'd gone deaf," said Charles, "and God, I'm already blind."

My wife had a great uncle, Blind Bill Smith of Buchanan

County, VA, who was a locally famous piano player. Like Doc Watson, Blind Bill sometimes tuned pianos for a living. He was notoriously hard-living, for a man with such a disability, until he found Jesus late in life. It was an experience he related to his brother in a series of letters I'm still reading.

"It is true that I have missed the beauties of this world," Blind Bill wrote home, "but it is great to know that I will see in a world that is more beautiful than this one."

Blind Bill's letters made me reconsider Doc Watson. Did Doc feel that he missed the beauties of this world? To me Doc Watson *was* one of the beauties of this world. I'd never mention his handicap—Doc preferred to call it "a hindrance"—if I didn't feel a trace of guilt. A great blind musician may be one of the few members of the human race who gives a lot more to the world than he ever gets back.

We're a selfish audience. We're the ones who benefit because Doc Watson had so much time to practice, so few distractions and temptations compared with Hank Williams or George Jones.

Watson was born the same year as Hank Williams, 1923—Doc was six months older. Country music has a history of cautionary tales, of stars who killed or lobotomized themselves with whiskey and drugs, or peaked early and spent their last forty years impersonating themselves on the Grand Ole Opry, singing the same three songs. So many of the great ones left us wishing they could have left us more. As much as he hated the life on the road ("the loneliness . . . but I had a family to feed"), Doc paid his dues and minded his music, and he outlasted them all.

We got our money's worth out of Doc Watson. Did Doc think it was a fair exchange, all things considered? I never asked him. I'm shy around people I admire, and musical geniuses make me, a non-musician, feel like a tourist. I only introduced myself, and shook Doc's hand, on one occasion. He was in Greensboro to receive one of his many folk arts awards, and I found him sitting alone in a classroom behind the stage area, waiting for an escort.

I don't think he heard me come in. It was an unfair advantage to take, but I watched him for five minutes before I spoke. It wasn't much of a conversation—two polite strangers, each caught out of his element in a different way.

If you wanted to hear Doc wax effusive, I was told, you started by praising Merle. Doc Watson's long, much-honored late career was an Indian summer any artist would envy, but it followed a hard, hard frost. The defining tragedy of Doc's life was the death in 1985 of his only son Merle, a superb slide guitar player who rolled a tractor over on himself one night up in Watauga County.

It was Doc's relentless grief that generated the Merle Watson Festival, which has convened in Wilkesboro, NC, every April since 1988. Though it's grown tremendously in size and renown, Doc never let his huge picnic lose its focus as a memorial to his son. In four days at Wilkesboro, you'll hear the name Merle a thousand times.

Merlefest, as they call it, is unique. It's not a fiddler's convention or a folk festival. It's more of a family reunion, a gathering of the clans where the names of the dear departed—not only Merle Watson but Bill Monroe and Carter Stanley and Mother Maybelle—are heard far more often than any names from the charts.

Merlefest is about remembering, about respect for your elders. It was inspiring to watch kids like Iris DeMent and Alison Krauss sing with Doc for the first time ever. Or to hear the late Guy Clark—looking none too well-preserved himself—sing the songs he wrote in honor of Doc Watson and Ramblin' Jack Elliott, legends of a previous generation who were sitting in back of him, grinning.

Up on his mountain, Doc was the man. Every April the country aristocracy, the best musicians from Nashville and the bluegrass circuit, came to the mountain to say "We love you, Doc." And God knows to hear him perform. A musician can tell you whether Doc Watson was always unchallenged king of the flat-pickers. The miracle, to me, is that Doc was singing better in the twenty-first century than he was two decades before. Whatever it took to temper and refine that warm honey baritone—age, grief, singing in the dark—his big voice was often the best one on the program. "A voice pure as mountain water," one critic wrote when Doc was eighty.

Flatlanders would come up to Wilkesboro to buy nostalgia—"Is he still performing?"—and go away raving about Doc's voice and the incredible range of his repertoire. Doc loved to rock, they were surprised to learn. He spent the '50s playing electric guitar in a dance band, and rockabilly suited him fine, especially Carl Perkins's "Blue Suede Shoes."

Doc Watson had more friends than The Library, and folklorists called him "a national treasure," which was no exaggeration. People might think that Doc Watson had a lot to be proud of, a lot of reasons to sing praise. But we can't ever know how another man feels about his luck, any more than we can know how he felt playing for ten thousand people he couldn't see. Maybe those festivals we loved just reminded him of how much it hurt to lose his boy.

Doc played his last Merlefest in April 2012, and I heard his last performance, at the Sunday morning Gospel Hour with the Nashville Bluegrass Band. One of the hymns he sang was "Heaven's Bright Shore." He died a month later, after a fall at his home in Deep Gap. He was eighty-nine. It takes another musician to eulogize a great one. These are only a fan's notes—but I despise that word, *fan.* It's a low-country, Disneyland kind of word, spawned by mass entertainment. They don't talk about fans in Deep Gap. Dock Boggs and Tommy Jarrell, Clarence Ashley, they had friends, neighbors, and appreciative audiences. They didn't have "fans." Hank Williams had fans, and Elvis Presley—and look what happened to them.

I never cared a lot about celebrity; I'm fascinated by people who do something difficult incredibly well. I've become deeply attached to just a few, and my sorrow is that I end up praising too many of them after they're dead. Doc was one of them, one of the best. This is nothing like an obituary that an editor assigned me to write. It's a personal appreciation by an admirer who's trying to say thank you, the only way he knows how.

Acknowledgments

"In Memoriam Thomas Hardy" from *New Collected Poems: Charles Tomlinson*, Carcanet Press Limited, 2009, used by permission.

Some of the essays in this book were previously published in slightly different form in the following publications.

"That's all she wrote: Remembering Molly Ivins." *Indy Week*, March 14, 2007.

"Master Historian" (John Hope Franklin). *Oxford American*, Issue 61, Summer 2008. Best of the South, Vol. III.

"A Farewell to Arms." *Gather at the River: Notes from the Post-millennial South*. Foreword by Louis D. Rubin. Louisiana State University Press, 2005.

"The Last Wolverine: James Dickey." *Cathedrals of Kudzu: A Personal Landscape of the South*. Louisiana State University Press, 2000.

"Confession, dedicated to a fighting nun." *Indy Week*, January 14, 2004.

"A Man of the World" (James Still). *Oxford American*, Issue 41, Fall 2001. Also collected in *Gather at the River: Notes from the Post-millennial South*. Foreword by Louis D. Rubin. Louisiana State University Press, 2005. Also collected in *James Still: Critical Essays on the Dean of Appalachian Literature*. McFarland, 2007.

"Son of a Preacher Man: Marshall Frady (1940–2004)." *Gather at the River: Notes from the Post-millennial South*. Foreword by Louis D. Rubin. Louisiana State University Press, 2005.

"Kirk Varnedoe, A Fine Disregard." *Creative Loafing* Atlanta, July 15, 2004. Also collected as "A Prophet from Savannah" in *Gather at the River: Notes from the Post-millennial South*. Foreword by Louis D. Rubin. Louisiana State University Press, 2005.

"In Memorium: Tommy Thompson, Father Banjo." *Oxford American*, Issue 45, April 2003. Southern Music Issue, Vol. VI. Also collected as "The Last Song of Father Banjo" in *Gather at the River: Notes from the Post-millennial South*. Foreword by Louis D. Rubin. Louisiana State University Press, 2005.

"Judy Bonds (1952–2011)." *Oxford American*, Issue 72, Spring 2011.

"The Last Southern Hero." *Cathedrals of Kudzu: A Personal Landscape of the South*. Louisiana State University Press, 2000.

"Will David Campbell (1924–2013)." *Oxford American*, Issue 82, Fall 2013.

"Requiem for a Bantamweight." *Oxford American*, Issue 24, November/December 1998. Also collected in *Cathedrals of Kudzu: A Personal Landscape of the South*. Louisiana State University Press, 2000.

"But Now I See, Doc Watson's Gifts." *Oxford American*, Issue 27/28, Summer 1999. Also collected in *Cathedrals of Kudzu: A Personal Landscape of the South*. Louisiana State University Press, 2000.